So You Want to be a Company Director

By Warren Tapp

Disclaimer: *Although every care has been taken to ensure the correctness of information and opinions provided in this book the author specifically disclaims responsibility for any errors, mistakes or incorrect facts or interpretations which may occur, however caused, and accepts no liability on any basis. Comments and recommendations made in this book are not to be construed in any way whatsoever as legal advice. Readers should seek their own professional advice before acting on any advice or opinion in this book.*

Published in Australia by Sid Harta Books & Print Pty Ltd,
ABN: 34632585293
23 Stirling Crescent, Glen Waverley, Victoria 3150 Australia
Telephone: +61 3 9560 9920, Facsimile: +61 3 9545 1742
E-mail: author@sidharta.com.au

First published in Australia 2023
This edition published 2023
Copyright © Warren Tapp 2023

Cover design, typesetting: WorkingType (www.workingtype.com.au)

ISBN: 978-1-922958-22-8

About the Author

Warren Tapp has had extensive experience over many years as a company director and as a consultant to boards in Australia and overseas. He has been a director of more than two dozen companies in the last thirty years and at one stage was the non-executive chairman of seven boards in Australia and overseas. For more than ten years he facilitated modules on the company directors' course for the Australian Institute of Company Directors and has been a keynote speaker at many conferences in relation to corporate governance and the role of the board.

His qualifications include an MBA as well as a Master of Laws and a Graduate Diploma in Applied Corporate Governance. He has also completed the advanced company directors' course and number of short courses conducted by the AICD.

Warren is a fellow of the Australian Institute of Company Directors. Now semi-retired, he is still serves as a non-executive director while completing further postgraduate studies. He lives on the Gold Coast in Queensland.

Introduction

can't count the number of people who have asked me how they can become a member of a board and what is actually involved. For some years I therefore saw a need for a book to provide some of the answers but only now have I found the time to put pen to paper. I thought such a book would help those many people who are considering joining their first board or who may already be a director without really understanding what they should be doing.

While there are hundreds of books available on corporate governance they tend to be textbooks explaining complex legal or accounting matters. There is nothing to help someone understand the fundamentals of being on a board of directors or that shares the knowledge and experience about the life of a director.

So, you want to be a company director? I hope this book gives you some insights into what it involves.

Warren Tapp

Contents

The Author v

Introduction v

Chapter 1   *Why Do It?* 1

Chapter 2   *Getting On Boards* 17

Chapter 3   *Induction* 33

Chapter 4   *Corporate Structures* 43

Chapter 5   *Legal Matters* 59

Chapter 6   *Finances* 75

Chapter 7   *Risk Management* 85

Chapter 8   *Strategy* 95

Chapter 9   *The CEO* 109

Chapter 10   *The Chairman*.............................127

Chapter 11   *Director Dynamics* 133

Chapter 12   *Board Papers* 145

Chapter 13   *Committees*.................................157

Chapter 14   *Board Meetings*..........................167

Chapter 15   *Board Performance* 175

Chapter 16   *Professional Development*...........189

Chapter 18   *Not-For-Profits* 207

Chapter 19   *Getting Off*.................................221

Chapter 20   *Why We Need You*......................229

Chapter 1
Why Do It?

f you have never been a company director and you are considering joining a board, then you should ask yourself 'why do it?'

There are many reasons people join boards that may answer the question for you. For example, you have been approached by a company which is looking to fill a vacancy on its board and has asked you to consider taking up that appointment.

It may be that you have been asked to represent a significant investor to be their nominee director in the company in which they have invested.

It may be that a family-owned business wishes to appoint new directors who may be family members or independent directors themselves.

It may be that you've decided that at this stage in your career it would be interesting to join a board quite apart from your current full-time work role or it may be that you are looking to develop a portfolio of positions with the aim of becoming a full-time professional director. Whatever the reason, you need to think seriously about why you would want to do it.

Some people have a false view that it is a well-paid position that only involves a meeting once a month if that. I know of others who have accepted board appointments because they felt there was some prestige attached and it would look good on their CV. Others have joined a not-for-profit board because they really wanted to do something worthwhile in the community. Some younger people have joined the family company board because dad has told them they don't have any choice.

In my view, there is only one reason you should do it and that is because you believe you have the skills required and can make a real contribution to the company and its shareholders. You really have to enjoy the role of a director so that you have a passion for it.

There are those who see it as some kind of invisible club these people belong to and nobody else could join.

No doubt that was a perception people once held which probably wasn't true . There is no doubt that the role of a company director has changed enormously from those days.

The high-profile corporate collapses of the '90s and the noughties have resulted in major reforms to the Corporations Law and the subsequent responsibilities of company directors and the expectations of people in that role. When I see the difficult times that some directors have had to cope with over the years and the increasing risk of liability one has to wonder why anybody would want to do it.

We read annual reports that talk about chairmen of major Australian public listed companies earning hundreds of thousands of dollars a year in fees. However, we don't very often hear about the directors with the same level of responsibility working extremely hard for small to medium companies for annual fees that probably equate to less than $20 an hour.

If you happen to be appointed as chairman of a board, you will find you will need to contribute many more hours because of the unique responsibilities of that role. This is on top of the fact that sometimes it's rather like herding cats.

So how much time is involved?

This depends on the type of company, how big it is and what is happening to it at the current time. The amount of time required would be much less if you are a director of a small private company that is reasonably well established and not facing any major issues. There is much more time involved if you are a director of a major publicly listed company involved in takeovers or one with significant corporate problems requiring more of the board's attention. In my experience, directors for not-for-profit boards are often asked to be a lot more hands on and to help with such issues as fundraising and marketing over and above their corporate governance responsibilities.

In a typical company, a director can expect to attend a board meeting each month, which will last for at least half a day, if not longer. On top of that, they will be expected to participate in an annual budget planning session as well as an annual strategic planning session and any other special board meetings or other events. If the board has committees, you can expect to be on at least one of those which will involve three or four other meetings a year, quite apart from your main board meeting. You may be expected to attend other company functions throughout the year and perhaps travel to various sites around the country where the company has its operations.

All of this is apart from reading the monthly board papers and quite often a large volume of other material that is provided to you throughout the year relevant to your company. Then there is the annual general meeting which can be an interesting event depending on the shareholder makeup.

If you are also the chairman, you will need to communicate with the chief executive officer on a regular basis by phone or email, as well as spending time with individual members of the board to discuss issues between board meetings and also be an ex officio member of all board committees.

As chairman, you will also liaise with the company secretary on a regular basis in relation to the agenda and minutes for board meetings and any flying minutes (circulating resolutions). You will probably be also expected to keep your professional knowledge up to date by attending various courses or conferences and reading material regarding matters related to the trade or industry in which the company operates as well as corporate governance developments or changes.

Depending on the board policy in relation to conflicts of interest, you may also be required to disclose details of all your personal assets on a register of interests while at the same time knowing that those same assets potentially could be at risk as a result of any liability based on your actions as a director.

You will earn your fees if you are doing your job properly.

Some might wonder if they can get away with not spending much time in this role, leaving the CEO and chairman to pick up any problems missed by not attending meetings or reading all the material provided.

That is a dangerous attitude and we will see later when we discuss legal matters that you are exposing yourself to a high level of risk. High-performing boards will not appreciate a director who does not pull their weight and contribute. It is not hard for a good chairman to organise for the shareholders to not only appoint you but also remove you if you don't contribute.

I admire very much those willing people who volunteer their time as a member of not-for-profit boards or committees as they make a real difference to our community.

However, depending on a not-for-profit's corporate structure, you could find you have the same responsibilities and liabilities as those of a director of a major public company.

Fees may range from zero for a volunteer director, up to hundreds of thousands of dollars for a chairman of a major publicly listed company. Generally speaking, a non-executive director for most median-sized companies can expect to be paid somewhere between $25,000 and $50,000 a year in monthly instalments. A chairman generally receives between one-and-a-half and two times that fee because of the extra workload. Fees will vary depending on the size of company by turnover and staff numbers, as well as the industry sector and whether it is privately owned or government owned.

If you've been invited to join a board, you will usually be told the fees that you will be paid. Meanwhile you need to do your own research to try to establish what to expect in the way of fees, depending on the variables I have mentioned. In Australia there are a number of board consulting firms that who provide advice in relation to remuneration for non-executive directors and one or two of them conduct annual surveys and provide reports on fee levels which you can purchase.

Some of the well-known recruiting firms also have a reasonable idea of directors' fees based on their experience of filling board appointments. If you know any experienced company directors, you can ask them to share their knowledge of the current level of fees, but keep in mind they will vary depending on the industry and size of the business. On top of fees you should also expect the company to pay the premium for directors' and officers' liability insurance for all board members including yourself. There is usually no problem being reimbursed for any out-of-pocket expenses in the conduct of your role on behalf of the company, as long as it's been approved by the chairman, if that is company policy.

*   *   *

So, what is expected of you as a company director?

It's expected that you will attend all board meetings and not miss any because of 'other commitments.' Obviously, illness is a reasonable excuse, but other conflicting demands on your time should not be allowed to get in your way of attendance at board meetings or any other board activities. Good boards will usually work out the calendar for the year ahead so that you have the dates to put in your diary to avoid any conflict of time in the future.

You will also be expected to read all the board papers and any other material you are provided with throughout the year so that you understand fully all aspects of the company's activities. Depending on what the company is doing at the time, this can be a lot of reading. I can recall receiving 200-page reports analysing a particular project that the board had been asked to consider. That was in addition to the normal monthly reports.

You will also be expected to understand the information given to you. That means that you have a basic understanding of all the financial reports and realise what they mean as well as understanding any other technical reports or submissions, which can sometimes be quite complex. You will be expected to ask questions if you need more information or a better understanding of such information to ensure you are fully prepared to participate in decision making based on what you know. You will be amazed at the number of directors I have seen arrive at board meetings who had obviously not even read their board papers.

The board will expect you to consider all matters objectively and independently and base your decisions on purely what is in the best interest of the company and its shareholders. This may mean there will be times where you need to have an opinion different from the other directors, but you must be prepared to stand up for your point of view and argue your case strongly. It also means that once the majority of the board has reached a decision you accept that majority view and support it. You must be prepared to be a team player once everyone has had the opportunity to argue for or against a particular matter. Robust disagreement is a healthy thing around the board table, but it is not healthy once the board meeting is finished.

You must be also strong enough to not be railroaded by others around you, whether it is the chairman or the CEO, for example. If somebody is asking for a quick decision that you have not had time to consider fully, don't be afraid to ask for the matter to be postponed until later when you and the others have considered it fully or sought more information to support the case or proposal being put forward. You should also check the accuracy of the minutes from the last board meeting when you receive them and let the company secretary know if you believe they are not accurate.

You should be prepared to put time into attending company functions to meet the key stakeholders and ensure that any discussions with such people uphold the confidentiality that any board requires unless it is a matter already in the public domain.

You need to spend time considering the future strategy and financial position of the company so you can contribute actively to budget planning and strategic sessions held by the board. You should be willing to contribute any new ideas or thoughts for consideration by the board and CEO and introduce any contacts that you have that you believe will be helpful to the company. You also have to keep asking yourself, is the company acting in the best interest of its owners whether there is anything that can be done to add more value for the shareholders.

So why do it? In my experience it is to learn and understand that you can actually make a difference to a company and its owners. Any successful company is good for the nation because:

a. it creates employment;

b. it creates revenue for suppliers to the company;

c. it creates revenue for the shareholders through share price growth or dividends.

It also means that you may be part of a company that is doing something exciting in terms of its services, in what it makes and perhaps even exports.

It's given me great pleasure to know that I've been part of a team around a board table that over the years has seen a small business grow to a much larger one and make a real contribution to the economy through its turnover and taxes. For me it is a privilege to be allowed access to all the confidential information about a company that you need and be trusted to use that information in a proper way for the company and its shareholders.

That's not to say I have enjoyed every moment on the boards I've been on. I recall having some very heated ding-dong arguments with fellow directors over the years. I can also remember the times that I've had to tell a CEO their services are no longer required and realise the impact on that person and their family.

I've also shared the disappointment of years where we have not achieved the budget or financial outcomes we had hoped for. I can recall when the board and all its members were vilified in the press unfairly, but we had to cop it on the chin. There have been times where we have uncovered cases of fraud or embezzlement by management or staff resulting in police action.

I have attended shareholder meetings where there have been abusive remarks made to the directors for events that have been beyond their control. I have dealt with CEOs who have been less than cooperative with the board and sometimes rude and evasive.

It has been a great classroom for learning about people's behaviour. At the end of the day, we're all human beings and it takes all types to make up a board of management for any organisation. This is why you will also be expected to treat those around you with respect and make it clear that you expect the same in return.

There is one final another reason you should do it. This is because you can have a great deal of fun in a serious role if you have an open mind to the things around you. When I look back upon the various boards I've had the privilege of joining, I can remember many exciting times. These have included going over construction projects with a hard hat on and seeing a new road or bridge or building coming into being. I can recall being shown through large cargo ships and through bottling plants as well as the back of fast food retail outlets and many other interesting industries.

I can recall the pleasure of announcing record profits to shareholders at an AGM as well as the privilege of officially opening a new branch or factory or outlet in different capital cities or country towns. I recall with a smile on my face the many company conferences I have had attended over the years which have involved plenty of fun and games and the odd drink or two, as well as activities involving helicopters, jet skis, motorbikes and racing cars.

Finally, it's given me the pleasure of meeting some incredible people. These have not only been my fellow directors or senior managers, but all the staff of the many businesses with which I've been involved. To see the enthusiasm and passion some employees have really makes you proud to be part of that whole team.

I've also been on not-for-profit boards where the organisation has managed to make a real difference to people's lives and has gained the generous support of sponsors from all walks of life to help the cause we have been working for. That has also allowed me to meet many terrific volunteers who do so much for our community that people never hear about. All that enjoyment is on top of the pleasure of getting inside a company, understanding it, and trying to make a difference with your thinking and ideas, even though you may have never worked in that industry before.

A non-executive director does not necessarily have to be an expert in a company's particular industry. Instead, a good director ensures that the fundamental principles of corporate governance are followed, whatever type of company it is.

I'll talk about these fundamentals later in the book but at the end of the day, shareholders are trusting you to be the guardian of their vested interest in the company and it's a good feeling if you know you have got it right for them.

I hope these few thoughts will help you reflect on why you should be a company director. If you've thought about doing it, make sure it's for the right reasons and if you are already a company director, make sure you will still be doing it for all the right reasons.

Ask yourself whether you would still want to contribute to this company even if it didn't pay you.

Do you like this particular business and the people

in it and will you be allowed to make as much of a contribution as you can?

It's much the same test you should apply when asked to join a not-for-profit board. Do you feel you have the right set of skills needed to be a proactive member of this board or will you be going along for the ride as a passenger?

It's too late to learn how to be a company director once you're on a board. But it's not too late to learn how to be a better director while you're there. Boards make a valuable contribution to the national economy by leading and guiding companies to create more profits and employment and pay more taxes.

There are hundreds and thousands of companies, large and small, and they all need directors. I am probably biased, but I think it's an important role in society and there will always be a need for willing people to contribute their time, energy and skills around the board table. It doesn't matter whether that table is on the top floor of a city skyscraper or around the family kitchen table, directors do make a difference.

Chapter 2
Getting On Boards

I f you want to be a company director the first thing you need to work out is how you can be appointed to a board. For some people the invitation to join a board comes to them rather than having to go searching for a board appointment. This generally happens because they are either well-known from their experience on other boards or a company is in the middle of a set of circumstances that involves the need for a director to be appointed.

A family with its own company might be looking to appoint more family members to the board. Or it may be that you've been asked to represent an investor or shareholders as their nominee and they have approached you to accept a board appointment.

In the case of government boards, quite often a person will receive a call from a government department asking if they are interested in being considered by the relevant minister for a particular board appointment. In the case of not-for-profit organisations, I've seen people invited to join boards for all sorts of reasons. These have included such questionable steps as inviting anybody who makes a substantial donation to the organisation to become a director without any regard for the person's skills or ability.

It's also possible that your name is on the database or listed with a board consulting firm or headhunting organisation and that has contacted you to see if you are interested in a possible interview.

Apart from being invited to join a board, there are some steps you can take to be proactive in seeking board appointments yourself. Apart from the legal requirement to be at least eighteen years of age, no other prerequisite or qualification is required to become a director of a company. However, in recent years I have seen several boards looking for people who have at least completed the AICD company directors' course.

Let's assume that after reading the previous chapter you have decided you want to become a director for all the right reasons rather than the wrong ones. You have also checked that you have the time to commit to the role and there will be no conflict with your other activities or interests. So what now?

As already mentioned, there are businesses in most capital cities that provide a board consulting service. These often include a database of candidates who may be available for board appointments should one of its clients be seeking a non-executive chairman or director. You will find most of these in your local telephone book or you can Google either 'board consultants' or 'corporate governance' to see what names come up of organisations that specialise in your area. You could also find the contact details for most of the well-recognised recruitment firms.

Start with a telephone call regarding your interest in being included in their database and see if they have any specific requirements. Alternatively, write to them with a copy of your CV indicating your interest and availability. Some organisations allow you to register your details on their website rather than having to send a paper copy of your details.

They will not charge you to be included on their database; their clients pay them a fee to find the appropriate persons for their boards. As recently as twenty years ago it was rare for companies to use a third party to find potential directors, but I've noted an increasing trend for this approach in recent times. I suspect this is because boards need to be seen to be more transparent and professional in the recruitment of potential directors, rather than simply inviting someone they know. It's pleasing to see boards becoming more aware of the need to identify the skills they lack and then search specifically for someone with those skills to complement the rest of the directors. It may be that the company circumstances require someone with specific experience, perhaps in the preparation for a public listing or float, or experience in mergers and acquisitions. They may also be looking for someone with specific international experience if a company is about to expand overseas.

Your CV does not need to be too long or very detailed in relation to your entire working career. Instead, these organisations are looking for any experience with boards and perhaps any tertiary qualifications including the company directors' course I've already mentioned. You might say, 'If I have no past experience, how could I be considered?' Don't let this put you off as some boards will consider people without previous experience if they have other attributes that are important to them.

In your CV try to highlight any commercial experience you've had in specific areas that would be useful for any board and perhaps provide a brief covering note explaining why you are interested in a board appointment at this stage of your career. Companies are prepared more and more to recruit directors that live interstate from their operations, so you may wish to indicate your willingness to travel outside your home region if necessary or indeed overseas if required.

Having said all that, it's a fairly passive exercise as you are then left waiting for a call from one of these organisations looking for a potential director. It won't happen overnight and, indeed, it could be a long time between drinks. Nevertheless, it's worthwhile having your name listed with such organisations.

Also, if a member of the AICD, provide it with your details for listing on its website. AICD also issue to members a weekly email with a national listing of Director Opportunities you can apply for. Companies looking for a director with AICD membership can access that information on a confidential basis to consider all the available candidates. There may be a nominal annual fee to be included for these opportunities.

Most state and federal governments keep a list of available candidates for consideration for appointment to government boards. Some local governments also require independent directors for their corporatised entities from time to time. With this in mind I would suggest you forward your details to the Premier's Department in each state and to the Department of the Prime Minister in Canberra, as well as to the CEO of any local authorities relevant to you.

Phone to check with the various departments to confirm if these are the right places to send your details. In some cases it may be the Treasurer's office, at either a federal or state level, or they may direct you to other specific government areas for inclusion on other lists. When you consider the number of government-owned entities with boards of directors there are numerous opportunities for board appointments. Again, it is a passive step that leaves you waiting to be contacted. When that happens it means they want to meet with you for an interview and consideration along with other candidates. Ultimately it will be the chairman of a board together with one or two other directors who will meet the final candidates before deciding to make an offer. In the case of government boards, the filtering process will require final approval by the respective minister. All this will include reference checks so you need to be sure there is nothing in your background that would hinder any consideration for a board appointment and that you are not disqualified in any way in accordance with the Corporations Act.

These are all fairly passive steps but are necessary if you are to have your name out there in the right places. However, there is no doubt the most active step you can take is to let all your contacts know you are interested and available for possible board appointments. It's amazing how your network of contacts can extend well beyond that initial group to many other people that you may not even know.

*   *   *

We assume of course that your reputation is sound and that you are well regarded so that your colleagues would be happy to recommend you when they hear of opportunities. It may be that your immediate contacts are themselves on boards or own their own companies and may be interested in knowing that you would be happy to discuss a possible board appointment.

If you've never been on a board, it would be good to get some experience while waiting for that phone call. The way to do this is to contact as many not-for-profit organisations as you wish and indicate your willingness to be considered for a board appointment knowing that it will be on a volunteer basis, although in recent times larger not-for-profits have started to pay directors' fees.

However, it is important that you approach only organisations in which you have a genuine interest or where you feel you can make a contribution. At least this gets you some board experience and always reads well on your CV. Apart from letting your colleagues know of your interest in this area, there is no reason not to make a list of companies that you would like to be involved with and contact the CEO to indicate your interest in any future vacancies on their board.

If you've had no previous experience, I would suggest you contact only small to medium-size companies that are probably privately owned. It is very unlikely that any public company would be interested in considering you without any board experience.

There may be a business you know of in an industry that you have experience or at least an interest in. There is no harm in sending your details to the CEO indicating you would always be happy to discuss any opportunities that might occur. I suggest the CEO because in most cases you won't discover the chairman or other directors without searching through the Australian Securities and Investment Commission office (ASIC) which is often a board member itself.

Consider any organisation of which you are a member. This may be a credit union or other mutual organisation where the directors are appointed from within the membership. These often have paid board positions and it's useful for them to know of potential candidates for future nomination.

Depending on your work circumstances you may have a client list that you can approach and indicate your interest in their company and their board. Obviously one has to be careful with this depending on your current business relationship and the usual ethical issues. Meanwhile be happy gaining experience on any committees or boards of clubs or other organisations with which you are associated. There is no doubt the hardest step is being invited to join your first board as a paid director. Once that happens, it seems to open up invitations from other companies. As you gain more board appointments, you find more and more companies hear about you and approach you to consider their board.

Getting started is the hardest part, but be persistent in your efforts and be patient for that first phone call. Meanwhile consider what you can do to further your professional development to equip yourself even better as a suitable member of any board.

While companies tend to automatically like people with legal or accounting qualifications, it is useful to try to develop any other tertiary qualifications you can whether it be at graduate diploma level or a university degree. If you already have an undergraduate degree in some other discipline you could consider doing an MBA to round out your commercial skills. As already mentioned, AICD provides a wide range of courses at various levels, but specifically in the corporate governance field. If you are not particularly skilled in finance, you may consider doing some further short-course studies in this area as it is critical to your role.

*   *   *

Once you have been asked if you are interested in being considered for a board appointment, it's important to know the next steps in gathering more information about the company including where it is and what industry it is in and why there is a need to fill a board vacancy, although it may not be a vacancy, but simply a decision to increase the size of the board.

You should then arrange an initial meeting with person who contacted you. Don't ask about board fees at this stage, although you may be provided with that information at that initial interview. While they are assessing you, it's quite appropriate to ask more detailed questions to be sure that this is an opportunity worth further consideration Don't just grab the first offer that you receive, but be sure it is right for you and them.

Usually you will then be invited to meet the chairman or a selection committee or even the whole board. This will be the final step before they decide who they would like to offer a place on their board. You should use this as an opportunity to access the personality and style of the others around the board table to see if there are any potential problems you might be involved in should you join. Such problems include a dominant individual who expects everyone to simply be a 'yes' person or that their whole approach as a board is to pay only lip service to good corporate governance practice. If that's the case, the potential exists to bring you problems later.

At this meeting, you should also be prepared to ask what plans the board has for the company's future and how they see your role as a member of their team. It may also be an opportunity to meet the CEO to assess his/her style in relation to working with the board. Perhaps ask them for printed information that you can take away. This might include the company's brochure and some of its product literature as well as any information publicly available regarding the company's financial performance.

Try to do your research and homework on the company from this meeting to ensure you are comfortable about joining its board. Should you then receive an invitation to be appointed to the board, you should then insist on access to a wider range of information to conduct due diligence. This means that you review the company's financial position as well as any other relative information such as pending legal action against the company or other problems that might emerge once you join the board. Because your liability starts from the day you are registered with ASIC as a director of that company, you need to be sure you are not opening a can of worms.

You should obtain the chairman's permission to speak to the CEO or other directors if you need to clarify anything else before making a final decision about accepting the offer. You need to confirm that directors' and officers' liability insurance is in place or will be made available at the start of your appointment. You should also clarify the annual director's fees and any other benefits and reimbursement policy. It is at this time that you should obtain a clear agreement in writing regarding what is expected from you in relation to the number of board meetings or other activities throughout the year and any committees you will be expected to join as part of your board work.

Unhappy directors tend to occur when there is a lack of clarification regarding expectations of the board and of the appointee before either party finds out too late the situation is not what either party thought.

Most directors are appointed for a period of three years and are often then invited to be reappointed for a further three years and or even longer. It is rare that a director appointment is for only one year and I would question why the board has such a policy in its constitution.

So far I have talked about the board deciding which person to appoint. But you need to keep in mind that technically it is the shareholders who appoint the directors and this is usually done by nominating candidates for election by the shareholders at the annual general meeting. However, under most constitutions, a board does have the power to fill any vacancy during the year and it will often do this in order to ensure it has the candidate they want to stand for election at the AGM.

For smaller companies the shareholders are often not so active as the principal owner will generally decide who they would like on the board. In some not-for-profits, the CEO decides who should be on or off the board.

You may also have asked the chairman for the opportunity to talk to the CEO face to face and perhaps with one or two other directors individually. This allows you to gauge the kind of people you will be working with and thus make sure that you will be allowed to make a contribution and not be expected to simply sit there and say nothing. It is important that you are comfortable that the CEO understands the relationship between the board and their position and they don't think the tail wags the dog.

Once you have advised the appropriate people that you are happy to accept any offer, you should ask for a letter setting out the offer with all the terms and conditions agreed by both parties. You will usually be asked to sign a copy of the letter of offer to be returned to the company, while retaining a copy for yourself.

You will also need to provide a letter confirming your agreement to be a director of that company so this can be forwarded to ASIC together with the appropriate form required by them. You will then be officially recorded by ASIC as director of that company until further notice. You will have already negotiated the date for your first board meeting and have asked for confirmation of the dates for the rest of the year so you can lock them into your diary.

All this process can take one or two months if it's done thoroughly by you and the board that you are joining and if the board has a well-regarded reputation. This is not the same as applying for a job and any timetable you might have in becoming a director on one board, let alone a number, may take longer than you think.

Being a company director can be a bit like being a politician. There is no certainly about your tenure and you are at the whim of the voters or shareholders as to how long you stay. Any term of your appointment indicated in the letter of offer is always subject to the shareholders' wishes so don't give up your day job when you get your first board appointment.

Chapter 3
Induction

I t never ceases to amaze me how little induction is provided for company directors when they join boards. While most businesses organise extensive induction programs for new employees, this doesn't always seem to be the case for new directors who have the most responsibility in guiding the company's affairs.

As part of your due diligence I suggest you ask the chairman what induction will be provided should you join the board. If there is none, I recommend you ask for an induction program to be arranged to assist you.

Assuming you have completed your due diligence and have accepted the offer to join the board, you should be looking to receive as much information as possible well before your first board meeting. Once you are appointed legally as a director you are entitled to access any information regarding the company and nothing should be withheld from you. Part of your due diligence is actually part of your induction process as you will have already probably reviewed some of the following documents:

- The last three years' financial result;

- The last few months of board papers and minutes;

- Company literature, including information regarding what it does and its products and services.

Once you are officially a director, you should ask to meet again with the chairman to discuss any pending issues and to ascertain the protocols the board relies upon. You should also ask to meet with the CEO again and with any other key officers of the company to get a feel for some of the issues currently in place. They will provide further opportunity to gather information and understanding regarding the company's operations.

You should also meet with the company secretary to discuss any governance issues that are relative to the board at the present time. If you have not completed the company directors' course, then you may wish to ask the chairman for permission to attend the course at the company's expense within the next few months. You could also consider undertaking further professional development as soon as possible to increase your ability to make a greater contribution to the board's discussions.

If possible, make time to meet some of the other directors over a cup of coffee to get different views about issues and the company and some of the 'politics' that are alive and well. By this stage you are allowed to ask any questions regarding confidential company information that you have read to get a better understanding of any matters that cause you concern or that you need to clarify. It will be useful at this stage to confirm the dates of all board meetings for the coming year and any other activities so that you can put them in your diary to make sure that you are available to attend these events.

Some chairmen may tell you there is no formal induction process and you will have to learn on the job. If this is the case, be proactive in undertaking most of the research outlined earlier in this chapter so that you can get your feet under the table as soon as possible. As far as ASIC is concerned your liability starts from the moment you are appointed to the board and so it's important that you understand all the issues as quickly as possible. It will be no defence later to say that you were not aware or didn't understand the issues if they occurred early in your board appointment term.

A director needs to simply understand the key drivers for the company in terms of what may make it or break it. In other words, what are the key issues that will make the company more profitable and successful as distinct from those issues that can damage the company and its future sustainability. These factors will vary from industry to industry and from company to company. These are the factors you will need to focus on and to be ready to ask questions and make decisions on.

Your due diligence needs to confirm there are no issues of concern to you *before* you join the board as it will be too late once you are legally a director for events that occur even one day after your appointment. That is why it's important to do your research as thoroughly as possible and meet all the key stakeholders to understand any emerging or latent issues that will affect the company and its directors.

It is essential that you are as fully briefed as possible before you attend your first board meeting rather than turning up and trying to understand exactly what's happening during the meeting. Experience has taught me that you should not say too much at your first board meeting but look and listen to see how the players operate around the board table and how issues are discussed and decided. By all means express an opinion if you have already formed one and don't be afraid to vote on any resolution the board has to make based on the any knowledge you have already gained.

Your due diligence should have confirmed that you have a chairman who is fair and who will allow all directors to have their say and that there are no other directors who want to dominate the conversation or not listen to your point of view. The rest of the board don't expect you to be up to speed at your first meeting and you won't wish to embarrass yourself with unnecessary questions that can be answered outside the board meeting. While they don't expect you to know everything, they do expect that you will not bog the meeting down with minor details or petty questions that you can get answered outside the meeting.

The best advice for your first board meeting is the old saying about people having two ears and one mouth for a very good reason. Feel free to take a lot of notes during the meeting so that you can reflect on these later. Remember, however, that the meeting is not the place for you to learn all the things that you can find out outside of the meeting. By the second meeting, however, you should be in a position to start asking useful questions and to express considered opinions on issues about the company and its operation.

Be careful not to focus on an area that is your particular skill as you are expected to consider a wide range of matters as a director. For example, if you are an accountant, you don't ask questions only regarding the finances and ignore every other matter. Similarly, you have a human resource or a marketing background, you don't try to look like an expert in these matters because of your particular qualification or skill. Instead you should be looking at the company as an overall entity and be able contribute meaningful input on a wide range of subjects.

Further, if you do have a particular qualification or

skill, you need to make sure that you have not been recruited to the board solely because of that skill and be expected to be the in-house expert on that matter as the board should seek outside professional advice on matters rather than rely on the expertise of any one director. You are not there to be the in-house expert on a particular matter, but rather as a director for the good of all shareholders or members. This doesn't mean that you can't offer a considered opinion based on your expertise on a particular matter, but don't let the board assume that is the only area you're able to contribute to with your opinions or decisions.

Spending the first couple of months really getting to understand the company and all the issues affecting it involves talking to a wide range of management, staff, fellow directors and key officers as quickly as possible. It may also mean reading a large volume of further material that you did not require in your due diligence process. Spend time in meetings with the CEO and other key people to be briefed fully on all areas of the company to expand your knowledge and understanding. The first board meeting should give you a very good feel for the protocols and politics of the board so that you know how to fit in as a team member while retaining your independence of thought as a member of the board.

If this is your first board appointment, it may be useful to talk to other directors with some experience to get their ideas regarding the best way to be fully inducted and up to speed in your role. From a legal point of view, a non-executive director is not expected to have the detailed information regarding every aspect of operations as possessed by the management or staff. Therefore your induction does not require you know how to do the job of every person in the organisation, but simply what the key drivers are in the company. Be careful not to get dragged into some of the existing politics of the organisation, but try to remain aloof and objective at all times.

I have seen chairmen or CEOs try to influence a new director very strongly towards a particular line of thinking to get them inside their tent. Watch out for this and listen politely to their points of view but take time to form your own judgement regarding what is in the best interests of the company and its owners. Some boards will have already formed factions or sub-groups that tend to follow a particular point of view versus the rest of the board. Be careful not to be dragged into one of these sub-groups or factions but try to remain independent or aloof and outside any particular cliques.

As stated earlier, it can take a new director as long as a year to get their feet under the table, which is why they need a three-year appointment to make a meaningful contribution. This does not mean you should take the whole twelve months to understand the key drivers. The reality is you will be more effective after a year than you will at your first board meeting. By the end of the first year you will be talking their language and understanding the key issues and will have seen how the players operate around the board table and in management.

You might ask if you can attend any industry conferences or trade shows or be put on the subscription list for any industry magazines or publications so that you have an opportunity to really understand the industry in which the company operates. If you can get access to any data or information on competitors in the industry this will broaden your knowledge.

As I said at the beginning of this chapter, most companies don't seem to have a formal induction process for new directors so it will be largely left up to you to be proactive in getting your feet under the table as quickly as possible.

Despite this, there will be issues about which you won't have a full understanding, even one or two years after joining a board. This can be despite your best efforts to get your head around all the major issues. I have found a year or two later matters arise in board papers that are new to me and I've had to make enquiries well before the board meeting so that I understand what the board is being asked to consider for the first time since I joined it.

Finally, remember that the shareholders are not paying you a fee to learn the job. They expect you to start looking after their interests as quickly as possible. I suggest your induction process should start from the moment you accept an offer to join a board and not during or after the first board meeting.

Chapter 4
Corporate Structures

For those of you with little knowledge of companies in Australia, it might be useful to summarise corporate structures and where directors fit into these models.

The simplest business operation is a sole trader. This is a person who operates without any incorporated entity around them and therefore assumes personal liability for anything that happens to their business. They usually pay tax at a personal marginal rate and probably have a business name registered with the Office of Fair Trading.

If more than one person decides to start a business, they will quite often form a partnership. A lawyer will draw up a partnership agreement which allows the unincorporated entity to earn revenue and split the profits after expenses. The bad news about such structures is that each partner is jointly and separately liable for any actions of the other partner, including the debts left behind the partner who has gone to South America! Be very careful about entering into such a formal business partnership and even more so about doing it with family members or very close friends. Too many times I have seen the heartache and disruption caused when things have gone sour.

The reason most people form a company is because their accountant has indicated that their sole trader marginal tax rate is now well in excess of the company tax rate and so they will be better off in a company structure. The accountant can usually arrange a shelf company within twenty-four hours and suddenly the sole trader becomes a director of their own company and probably as the main shareholder.

A company is like a separate person in that it has legal rights, just like you and me, and the directors are simply the people who provide the mind or brain for this entity in directing its affairs. Bear in mind that the assets and bank accounts of the company need to be kept separate from that of the owner, even though it is their company. Too often I have seen husbands and wives become the directors of a company in which the wife has no active business role but still has the same liability as any other director in Australia.

Try to avoid silent or sleeping partners becoming directors of a company if you don't want them to have the risk that goes with the job. There are number of law cases that confirm the court's view that such people have no excuse when things go wrong.

It's possible to have a single-shareholder and single-director company and generally these are very easy to operate. A good accountant will help you complete the minutes required for statutory returns and you will not require an audit of the company's affairs but simply to lodge a company tax return each year.

You may have more than one shareholder and more than one director and a proprietary limited company is a common small business entity. However, if the business expands, you have to be careful that you don't fall across the threshold of becoming what is deemed a large proprietary limited company. This requires the company to be audited and generally more closely monitored by ASIC which is the regulator or policeman for company affairs in this country.

The relevant thresholds are:

- $25 million in revenue;

- $12.5 million in assets;

- 50 employees.

If you have fewer than this in two out of these three thresholds, you are deemed a small company and if you have more than this in two out of three thresholds, you are deemed a large proprietary limited company. Your accountant will advise you regarding these matters and your obligations as a director of the company.

Every company requires a company secretary and if you are a sole director you are also the company secretary and therefore the public officer as far as ASIC is concerned. As the company grows, the role of company secretary becomes more important and may eventually require the services of a professional company secretary or key staff member to undertake this role in more detail. (Generally speaking, corporate structures are very similar in New Zealand and most of what is discussed in this chapter has relevance to directors in that country as well.)

Eventually a company may require more capital and therefore invites more investors to become shareholders. Once you have a number of shareholders, ASIC takes a greater interest in your company. You are then regarded as a public unlisted company and you will be required to hold annual general meetings for the shareholders and audit the company's affairs. You will also need to communicate with shareholders more frequently than you would in a small private company and so the company secretary role becomes more important.

Ultimately you may decide to list the company on the Australian Stock Exchange, which means the shares in the company can be bought and sold in the marketplace by the general public. Note that being a director of a public listed company becomes far more onerous. For example, there is a requirement under the Corporations Act for you to give notice of any intention to buy or sell shares in the company yourself and there will be certain times throughout the year to be allowed to do this. The board also needs to ensure continuous disclosure of any event affecting the market price and there are severe penalties for the directors and the company if this is not done in a timely manner.

Apart from this, be prepared to have your name in the media on a regular basis, depending on what is happening with the company and its activities. On top of that, you will need to attend an AGM each year and listen to shareholders who may not be happy about returns you are providing them.

A public unlisted or listed company requires a minimum of three directors, two of whom must be resident in Australia. A proprietary limited company requires a minimum of one director, of which one must be resident in Australia. If you are not clear about the size of your shareholder register by number, you need advice from lawyers or accountants to confirm what is the status of your company and therefore your relevant obligations as a director of that entity.

Other types of companies include joint venture entities and companies with nil liability operating in the mining sector. Some companies are guaranteed by members and shares and others by shares only. However I won't go into the detail of these as they are very specific to some directors.

In the not-for-profit area, many organisations

are unincorporated associations. This means they are simply a gathering of people with a common interest such as a charitable purpose or sporting or recreational interest. There is no incorporation and the liability remains with all the members in this particular group. Such a group is not able to enter into contracts or have any legal status in itself, as it is simply a gathering of people.

In Australia, most not-for-profits eventually become incorporated in one of two ways. In most cases they apply for approval to become an incorporated association. These are regulated in each state by the respective state legislation, usually through the Office of Fair Trading. Generally, they are not allowed to operate outside the state where they are incorporated and they are a low-cost and simple means of providing an incorporated structure for not-for-profit organisations. They will operate with a constitution usually referred to as the model rules and require a management committee of president, secretary and treasurer, as well as other committee members. The penalties for breaches of the relevant state Act are fairly small to avoid discouraging volunteers taking on such committee roles for the good of the community.

An incorporated association is required to submit annual returns to the state regulator and requires their approval for any changes to their model rules or other ways of operating outside of the system that has been approved in the first place. Because it is an incorporated entity, it does provide some protection to the members and it has the legal right to enter into contracts and undertake debt, et cetera. The management committee must act in the interest of all the members in order to meet the objectives of the association that are enshrined in the original model rules or constitution of incorporated association.

Unfortunately, I have found that quite often these well-meaning volunteers have not been prudent in their governance of the organisation and many have fallen into financial difficulty and in some cases cease to exist altogether. If you are asked to join the committee for an incorporated association, I suggest you undertake the same level of due diligence you would in joining any board and make sure that the committee knows what it is doing in running the organisation.

The other type of entity for not-for-profit is a company limited by guarantee.

This means that the members that own the company will guarantee the debt of the company up to a nominal amount set out in the constitution should it become insolvent. Because this is a member-based company, it will not be allowed to pay dividends from any profit or surplus it makes, but must ensure that such proceeds are spent on furthering the company's objectives for the benefit of all its members. This entity is regulated under the Corporations Act by ASIC and the board will consist of directors with the same level of liability as a director of any other company in the commercial world.

If you don't get paid as a volunteer director of such an entity, this is no excuse regarding your responsibility to know what you are doing at all times. A not-for-profit entity like this may choose to pay its directors a nominal feel or honorarium, but in most cases you are doing it for the good of the organisation. As much as you want to contribute to the community, if you are invited to join the board of such an entity, make sure you do the same degree of due diligence that I have set out previously. Be sure that you're not being asked to join the board because others think you'll be good at fundraising or getting donations as that is not necessarily the role of a director.

You should be prepared to do a little more than on a commercial board in terms of helping with operational matters, but don't be distracted from your prime responsibility of looking after the company and its interest on behalf of all the members. It's no good if you've sold the most raffle tickets in the month only to find at the next board meeting the company is insolvent. I will talk more about not-for-profit boards later in the book.

*   *   *

In summarising the topic of corporate structures, I would like to leave you with a simple model that I have always found useful. I call it the power hierarchy.

If we understand that the first stakeholders in the corporate structure are the owners (whether shareholders or members), we realise these are the people who have the reason for the company to be created and exist. Often, because there are so many of these people, they will appoint a small group of people to represent their interests as their 'agents' and these are called directors. This board will be given the power to look after the company on behalf of the owners and act in the owners' best interests at all times. In other words, they are being trusted to do the right thing by the people who appoint them to look after the company's affairs.

The details of such authority are usually outlined in the company's constitution. This is a document I suggest you ask to look at as part of your due diligence before joining any board. A constitution is the contract between the owners and directors and is the document that provides the authority or power for the directors to act on behalf of the shareholders or members. It's also a document that I believe any board should have reviewed every couple of years with the view to making recommendations for improvements or changes with shareholder approval at any AGM.

In most cases the directors don't work in the business day to day and so they appoint a person to run the company on their behalf. This person is the chief executive officer and may be given a range of titles depending on the circumstances. This could include managing director or CEO or general manager. Keep in mind the first of these will be a voting member of the board, whereas the last of these reports to a board and has no decision-making ability with the board. In turn, this CEO is given the authority to hire other people and set up a reporting structure below them that provides cascading authority down to the most junior person in the organisation.

So you can see that the ultimate power remains with the owners who delegate their authority to the directors, who in turn delegate it to the CEO, who in turn delegates it to other managers and staff within the organisation. It's important to note that the power flows from the top down and any dysfunctional board generally is caught up when the power has either bypassed any of these players or even flows upwards and therefore in the wrong direction.

Often have I seen cases where shareholders start telling managers how to run the business when they have no right to do so. I have also seen CEOs having the ultimate say when the board is weak and simply a rubber stamp for a dominant or strong CEO.

In family companies I've seen a grandfather or a younger son having the most say for some reason with the directors being left almost powerless. In not-for-profit organisations I have often seen a CEO running everything and the well-meaning volunteers simply going along with his/her recommendations. In all these cases, this is a dangerous and dysfunctional model that should be avoided.

Always remember the role of a director is to represent the interests of all the shareholders or members and act in the best interests of the company. Generally the board is given wide-ranging powers to govern the company and it should ensure it is in control rather than letting other people above or below them hijack the company's affairs.

You can see why you need to do your homework before accepting any offer to join a board, whether it be a commercial entity or a not-for-profit organisation. If any of these dysfunctional issues exist, think very carefully before deciding to jump in. You will probably not find so much of a problem with public listed companies or even public unlisted companies as they generally have more mature and well-running governance. But it's best to find out first.

I would also suggest that you forget any ideas that you can join the board with a view to changing all this and making it right. In my experience you can spend so much time fighting these bushfires that you're not left with any opportunities to look after the affairs of the company overall. Be sure exactly what the rules and the expectations are so you are not left as the local bunny holding the can under the Corporations Act. You also need to be sure that they don't expect you to do as you are told in your capacity as a director if it conflicts with your legal duties and responsibilities.

You may find you're asked to join the board of a holding company and at the same time be appointed to some of its subsidiary company boards. Without providing a detailed legal explanation, make sure you understand the roles in relation to the duty you owe to the company to which you've been appointed and any potential conflict with the parent or subsidiary company that you are also a member of at the same time. If you have completed the company directors' course, you will understand how this works. Otherwise get a good corporate lawyer to explain your obligations if you're put in this position.

The other type of entity that you may be asked to become a director of will be a government-owned corporation. State or federal governments may or may not be subject to the requirements of the Corporations Act. Generally, the owner will be the shareholding minister relevant to that industry or portfolio and the board will be expected to produce profits and dividends in a commercial setting for its government owner.

In most cases they will offer Crown indemnity to you as a director for which you need to get legal advice to ensure you understand exactly what this means in taking on such a role. Local government or councils also often set up as corporate entities and you may be asked to join a board for one of these and the rules will be the same as for any government-owned corporation. At the end of the day the law generally does not distinguish too much if you fail to fulfil your duties and responsibilities in any capacity on such a board.

If you require further information regarding corporate structures, there are many excellent textbooks available through either AICD or most bookstores to explain these in further detail. Alternatively, you can access the ASIC website for a simple explanation of corporate structures and their legal requirements. In addition Googling companies in Australia will usually provide a wide range of information to round out your knowledge.

Chapter 5
Legal Matters

t's important at this point that you understand some of the legal issues involved in becoming a company director. In the previous chapter I mentioned directors' duties and responsibilities a couple of times. What I am now about to tell you is not meant to scare you off but to make sure that you are fully aware of your legal position in taking on such a role in Australia or New Zealand.

I've already mentioned the Corporations Act in Australia sets out the rules for company directors (in New Zealand it's the Companies Act) and the Australian Investments and Securities Commission (ASIC) is the regulator or policeman of the legislation in this field.

I further pointed out that a director is accountable to the legislation, whether it be a single-director small company or a large public listed company or a not-for-profit company limited by guarantee. The law generally does not distinguish between these in ensuring that you fulfil your role in several important ways. The national economy is based on a belief that directors will run their companies in the best interests of their shareholders or members.

Once again, there are excellent textbooks available to provide in-depth knowledge about directors' duties and responsibilities.

Alternatively, you will learn about these in completing the company directors' course through the AICD or you can visit the ASIC website for more information. In simple terms there are two main legal duties you must fulfil at all times:

- that you act in good faith and in the best interests of the company and for a proper purpose'

- that you act with care and diligence at all times.

The first is like a job description for a company

director while the second is the performance benchmark for those job descriptions. There are a number of other duties outlined in the Act, such as the requirement to pay creditors and not trade when insolvent, but the two that I have listed are the main drivers of a director's level of duty and responsibility. Keep in mind that you are there to protect this entity called a company and to look after the interests of the people who own it, whether they are shareholders or members.

To act in good faith means you should try to do the following:

- act honestly at all times;

- avoid conflicts of interest;

- make no improper use of your position a director to the detriment of the company;

- make no improper use of information you obtain as a director to the detriment of the company.

While we all understand what it means to be honest, you have to be careful that you don't do things that the law may regard as dishonest acts that cause some disadvantage to the company or its owners. An extension of this is fraudulent activity, which a director must avoid at all times. While dishonesty may be a civil offence, fraud by any director will be regarded as a criminal offence.

Making no improper use of your position or the information you get as your capacity as a director simply means that you must not gain any advantage over anybody else because of the unique role that you fulfil. Insider trading is the most common wrongdoing in this sphere, but there are many other legal cases of people who have breached their duties in relation to such improper use. You are not there to gain a benefit for yourself, but to provide a benefit to the owners. You are also not there to cause any damage to the company in a financial or material sense and make any gain from this yourself.

The other issue about improper use of information is not so much what you may gain from it, but the very relevance of confidentiality. How often have I seen boards that can leak like a sieve because some director decides to disclose confidential information to other stakeholders such as competitors, the media or specific shareholders. You are expected to be trusted to keep board discussions and decisions confidential unless authorised for release by the entire board.

A common occurrence in my experience is the conflict of interest. This is where a director fails to understand that they are participating in a decision that will benefit them and not necessarily the company. The biggest failure is that those directors that have no moral compass to even see a conflict exists and so fail to declare it. You are required to indicate any conflict of interest where you will have some material gain from your participation in a board decision. This means you must declare it to the chairman and the board and avoid that part of the board meeting where the matter is being discussed by leaving the room. Even if the board agrees you should stay for the meeting, it is better that you leave the room until the matter is resolved and then return. You should certainly have no vote on any matter in which you have a material interest.

I should point out that the law extends this requirement to not only yourself but to your extended family or other participants with which you have some connection. It's perfectly legal for your own business to tender or bid for a contract with a company of which you are a director as long as the whole process is done in an open and transparent way and no advantage is provided to your bid or tender because of your role as a board member. You should also stay out of any decision made about awarding any bid or tender for such commercial work at the time that the board considers them. It would be advisable to ensure that the minutes record you were absent from the board meeting during any discussion or decision on the matter in which you have a related interest.

I mentioned the requirement for directors to ensure that all creditors of the company are paid and that the company does not trade while insolvent. It's important you monitor these financial matters because the directors can be legally liable the company's debts on a personal basis. In some cases, this can be a sufficient amount to wipe out the entire assets of some directors if they're not careful. If you are asked to give a director's guarantee on any debt or finance, be very sure you've considered the matter carefully before agreeing to do so.

An increasing trend in Australia is for class actions to be mounted by shareholders against the directors of their own companies. Generally these have been successful, resulting in large damages claims to be paid by individual directors. In addition, company directors can be sued by any number of interested stakeholders for a wide range of reasons.

Apart from this, ASIC can prosecute directors for breaches of the Corporations Act which can result in significant legal expenses in defending yourself until proven innocent or otherwise.

Your liability remains for seven years after you have ceased to be a director of the company for any events that occurred up to the day that you ceased to be a director. Sometimes events will occur that have been a result of your board's decision some years earlier and may lead to legal action against you long after you have left the board. For this reason, I always suggest you should ask for a deed of access from the company. This gives you the right to obtain records and financial information from the company after you have left the board if required by you in the defence of any legal action against you. The Corporation Act now provides this right, but I have always felt more comfortable having my own deeds safely locked away for the years ahead.

You will find that the constitution of most companies does provide indemnity for its directors and officers, but I would be concerned if this is the only protection you have should the company become insolvent with no cash or assets left to support you. For this reason, directors' and officers' liability insurance becomes very important in the life of the director. Your due diligence before joining a board should establish if it already has this in place and you should ask to see a copy of the policy to be sure that it is adequate. If it doesn't have it, you should insist on this being provided at company expense before you join any board.

Alternatively, you can take out your own policy listing the companies of which you are a board member, but this will be at your expense rather than that of each separate company. Get expert advice on such policies as they include a wide range of types of cover and exclusions as well extensions for various activities as a director if required.

Don't let the company shop around for the cheapest premium, but get good advice on the policy that provides the most protections for you and the other board members and senior officers. Ensure that it has an advanced payment clause which allows you to ask the insurance company to pay your legal costs in advance of any decision reached by the courts. This is better than paying it out yourself and trying to recover it from the insurance company later.

You may also ask the company to ensure it maintains such policies for at least the seven years after you have left the board as any such cover will expire once the policy is allowed to lapse. The policy will generally not name individual people, but provide blanket cover for all directors and officers, including yourself, plus some financial protection if you are innocent in performing your duties. These are held in the names of other family members or entities such as a trust.

This leads me to the second duty I mentioned earlier – to act with care and diligence. Until twenty years ago this was a fairly subjective test, but certain legal cases established some benchmarks to allow a court to decide if you have been careful and diligent. This 'reasonable person test' simply asks what any other director would have done under the same circumstances at the same time to act in the best interest of the company and its shareholders. If you did that, then you should be okay. But if it is clear that you did not do what any other reasonable person would have been expected to do in that role, you may be in trouble.

In other words, you can't be asleep at the wheel and

expect to be doing a job properly, yet I have seen many occasions where a director has obviously not been acting with care and diligence. These have included people arriving at board meetings and trying to read their board papers during the meeting without any idea of what is happening. It has included directors who have missed meeting after meeting. Some directors admit that they have no idea what issues are being discussed and don't understand the complexity of them. Despite this they will often vote without really knowing what they're voting on. Other directors have allowed themselves to be railroaded by either a dominant director or chairman or CEO and have agreed to decisions that are found to be commercially unviable later.

I had one director tell me that after three years on a board he still didn't really understand the business or how it operated. That was an indictment of the chairman and the board in letting him continue that way but was also a criticism of his inability to act with care and diligence.

There are several things you need to do to fulfil this legal duty:

- You read all the information you are given, no matter how bulky or onerous it may seem.

- You continue asking questions until you fully understand everything you need to know before being asked to vote on any issue.

- You make time to talk to other directors, management or staff to get your head around complex issues.

- You might need to seek a professional opinion from an expert on a particular matter to explain something to you to the best of your knowledge.

- You make sure you attend every board and committee meeting and participate in all board activities and company events so that you don't miss anything.

- You need to be aware of corporate governance matters by attending external courses or reading books to keep your knowledge up to date and current as they are constantly changing.

Changes may occur in governance legislation or accounting standards or in laws that relate to a particular industry in which you're involved. Government policy or rules may change and impact your company. Other external factors, such as the economy, will require you to act with even further care and diligence in understanding events around you. If your financial skills are not as strong as they could be you need to ask even more questions to ensure that you are monitoring the financial affairs of the company on behalf of its owners at all times.

You may need to have special briefings with the CEO or other senior management and other directors outside of board meetings so that you fully understand and appreciate all the issues that are occurring at any time in the company's life.

Finally, don't be afraid to ask questions either during the board meeting or outside the meeting to be sure you fully understand the implications of every matter you are being asked to decide on at any time.

From a legal point of view, ignorance is no defence and from what I've seen, most directors in Australia who have got into trouble have been in breach of their requirement to act with care and diligence. If you consider some of the well-known corporate collapses that have appeared in the media in recent years, you will realise the directors were probably honest and trying to do the right thing, but took their eye off the ball in terms of the amount of care and diligence they should have been applying. If your company has a full-time professional company secretary, then you should use that person as a resource to provide you with advice from time to time or ask them to point out to you at any time where a possible breach of legislation may occur.

Not that you would join a board full of 'cowboys' in the first place, but if you do find once you're there that one or two individuals don't seem to care about good governance standards, don't let yourself join them. It is important to retain your independence and objectivity and set your moral compass in relation to your duties and responsibilities.

I always found it easy to sleep at night when I was a member of several boards at the same time. This is because my central focus was on doing what I thought was the best for the company and its shareholders or members. This sometimes was in the face of extreme criticism or argument from fellow directors who did not see the same requirement. Keep in mind that you're not there for your benefit (apart from the professional fees you're paid) but for the benefit of the company and its owners.

This does not mean that the board will not make unsuccessful commercial decisions from time to time. The business judgement rule in the Corporations Act provides directors with some protection when they make unsuccessful commercial decisions that were clearly done in the best interests of the company and its shareholders at the time. The reality is that a board will have to take risks from time to time in some of the commercial decisions it makes, but hopefully they will be well-researched and calculated risks having considered all the facts available at the time.

As I said earlier, this chapter was not meant to paint the role of a director as high risk, but simply to explain the realities of the law by which directors must abide. It is important that you at least understand some of the basic legal requirements in your capacity as a director, particularly in relation to your legal duties and responsibilities. Having done that, set your moral compass for a clear path ahead and get on with making a useful contribution in your capacity as a member of the board. If at any time you are not sure what to do in relation to these matters, perhaps seek the guidance of the chairman who will hopefully provide advice in relation to the appropriate action that maintains the highest governance standards.

Chapter 6
Finances

once heard the role of a company director described as one of foresight and oversight. In other words, directors must have the vision to look to the future and plan the strategy, while at the same time overseeing the affairs of the company, particularly finances.

I am not an accountant, but I quickly realised I had to understand the finances well enough to be able to fulfil my legal duties of acting with care and diligence. Again, there are many excellent textbooks on how to analyse financial reports and the AICD runs courses on finance for non-accountants.

No doubt it is valuable if a board does include a qualified accountant. However, one must be careful that they don't look at everything through numbers and ignore the non-financial aspect of the company.

Part of your due diligence before accepting a board appointment will be to discover any qualified accountants working for the company in key roles and perhaps even meet with the external accountants or auditors to get their view on the company's financial affairs. In reviewing a typical set of board papers as part of your research before joining a board, look at the quality of the financial reports to decide if they are sufficiently thorough and well presented to give every director a full understanding of the financial state of affairs.

The type of financial reports will vary depending on the size of the company and the industry in which it operates. There are a few financial reports I need to keep my finger on the pulse. These are:

1. profit and loss statement;

2. balance sheet;

3. cash flow forecast.

For a not-for-profit company, the profit and loss will be known as the income and expenditure statement but it has the same reporting effect. It is a snapshot in time of the revenue for the company and the expenditure for the same period and it's usually for the previous month that the board is reviewing. Naturally the aim is to produce a profit each month, or a surplus in the case of a not-for-profit organisation.

I have always wanted to see the actual monthly revenue and expenditure and profit against the budgeted figures for that month and the year-to-date actual results compared to the budgeted year-to-date forecast. It may also include columns that show variations to budget either by dollars or percentages.

The other key figure to look for will be the gross profit and for some companies the cost of goods sold producing this result. You may also want to see the year-to-date profit for the same period last year to see whether the overall profit has grown compared to the previous year as well as its comparison against the budgeted result.

In the case of the balance sheet, this is simply a snapshot at the same point in time showing the assets and liabilities of the company together with the equity position of the shareholders and the net assets owned by the company. Again it's useful to see if the company is growing its net assets on a year-on-year basis, but the figure that I think is more important for a director is the current ratio. This is the comparison of current assets against current liabilities (i.e. those assets that can be made liquid within twelve months and the liabilities due within twelve months). Common sense would tell any director that it would be ideal to have these assets at least match the liabilities and preferably be in excess of them to allow some buffer for any devaluation or write-down of asset value.

Any accountant will tell you it's not always entirely critical that this ratio is positive, but it needs to be considered along with other financial information in relation to the solvency of the company. Directors must be able to form an opinion that the company is able to pay its debts as and when they fall due. The balance sheet also allows you to monitor any trends in relation to the debt to equity ratio to see if the company is growing in value or becoming further in debt over time.

Some financial reports will include a cash flow statement, which is a report on the cash that has come into the company and the cash that has gone out for the same reporting period in the previous month. While this is useful, I find a cash flow forecast to be more useful in monitoring the likely cash position of the company in the months ahead. A further solvency check that accountants will use is the cash flow test to measure whether the company has the available cash resources to meet any of its expenditure requirements in the near future.

I have always wanted to see cash flow forecasts extending for at least three months and probably six or further. If these are done accurately they will indicate the closing cash balance in the company's bank account at the end of each month for the near future. You are quite entitled to ask the CEO or financial controller about forthcoming major expenditure obligations and the company's ability to meet these at the required time.

The other two reports that tie in with this forecast will be aged receivables and aged payables. These tell you what money is owed to the company by its trade debtors and what bills have to be paid to trade creditors. The ageing of these reports indicates if there is a slowdown in being paid or in the company's ability to pay its own bills, all of which tie in with the cash flow position going forward.

Another report useful for directors for consider is a

summary of key financial benchmarks. These include several ratios or percentages to measure the health of company's finances against these benchmarks it wants to review each month that are relative to that particular company.

For example, you may want to include the reports on the return on assets or the return on equity or interest time cover or many other ratios relative to the company. Your internal or external accountant can provide advice on some of the ratios you wish to consider.

Even for non-accountants it is important to know and request that such financial information is provided to you and the board. It is also important that you know how to analyse such financial information to give you a clear understanding of the financial state of affairs. Your board may also decide to ask for other financial reports that are useful for its particular operation, so don't be afraid of suggesting further information that the board may find useful in monitoring the finances of the company.

Ensure you understand all the debt that the company has and the types of loans that it has and how and when they are due for payment. Watch out for long-term liabilities that may only be included in one line on a financial report, but which are major obligations even a year or two down the track.

While it's important to know what you need to know and ask for the information you want, be careful you don't become overwhelmed by large volumes of financial reports that are not necessarily relevant for the board's consideration. I've seen some board papers include reams of information regarding detailed operational financial matters that can hide the critical information you should be looking at. Don't just accept what management gives you in your board papers. Tell them what you want as a board.

The other matter to consider is audits. I have already mentioned that a small proprietary limited company does not need to be audited whereas a large proprietary company or any public company is legally required to be audited at the end of each financial year. This will be done by an external chartered accounting firm appointed by the board and I would suggest that the board meets with the audit partner from that firm at least once a year to review and discuss any issues found in their audit.

The audit process is an external independent check

on the financial reports to ensure the accuracy of those reports before they are submitted to ASIC by the deadline of the end of October each year. In my view, any audit report should come direct to the board and not via management, but you should seek management's response to the report once the board has considered it.

It may be appropriate for your board to establish an audit committee which acts on behalf of the entire board in providing contact with the external audit firm and reviewing the audit process on behalf of the board and making any recommendations.

The other task that an audit committee might undertake is that of an internal audit. This is different from an external audit as it is looking at the controls the company has in place to minimise the risk of fraud or embezzlement. You might be surprised at how many times I've found companies that have allowed only one person to sign all the cheques or transfer funds electronically to wherever they like.

I strongly suggest any audit committee includes a qualified accountant. If you don't have such a person on your board to be a member of that committee, the board is quite entitled to recruit on external accountant to its audit committee even if they are not a member of the board. Their knowledge and skill make the audit committee far more effective and it really only needs to meet two or three times a year.

I am not an accountant by any means but I have learnt what to look for in financial reports. Every director's job is to safeguard the financial affairs of the company on behalf of the shareholders and members and this means you must act with care and diligence in reviewing the information and ask questions until you are satisfied you understand fully the financial state of the company at any time.

In my experience, looking at information about a particular point in time such as the previous month is not always useful in itself. Instead, I have found that watching trends over a period of time gives a better indication of which way a company's finances are heading. Given that the board's job is to grow the wealth of shareholders, this means improving the net assets on the balance sheet and improving the profits in order to be able to pay dividends.

On that matter, the board has the discretion to set a percentage of profits after tax that can be made available for dividends and most companies seem to operate at around fifty or sixty per cent of such after taxed profit, but that may vary depending on circumstances in any year. The board can also decide not to pay dividends at all if it wishes to retain cash for working capital or for financial sustainability.

Note that dividends can only be paid out of profits or previously retained earnings and the board should only do this if it does not jeopardise the overall financial health of the company. However, recent changes to the Corporations Act now allow companies to pay dividends out of working capital and profits as long as assets exceed liabilities. To do so will require a change to the company's constitution.

I have often had directors tell me they don't really understand the financial reports and this is a very dangerous situation in terms of personal liability. If you want to be a company director and you're not an accountant, take the time to gain a basic understanding of financial reports and what they mean. There are severe penalties for directors who allow a company to trade while insolvent and you must act with care and diligence regarding the finances of the company at all times.

Chapter 7
Risk Management

have often been asked what the roles of a director are and those of a board. In my mind this breaks down to several functions. These include:

- Strategic planning

- Setting policies

- Risk management

- Hiring a CEO

- Monitoring

You will see risk management is included among these functions. For many smaller companies it is an area they ignore at their peril. It is important for any board to spend time reviewing the risks their company may face and a good board will include this on their agenda for every meeting.

What is risk management?

It is the process of anticipating unforeseen events and taking steps to minimise the chance of them occurring. These are events with the potential to damage the company in some way and the directors therefore have a responsibility to manage this risk as best they can. With this in mind it is important to try to establish as a board some lead indicators that will tell you the clouds are forming in a certain part of the company's operation that may become a major problem. This allows the board and management to take time to reduce or mitigate the risk if possible. It's no good having lag indicators that tell you a negative event has already impacted on the company. It's no good explaining to shareholders that you're busy cleaning up the mess when they will want to know why you didn't stop the mess being caused in the first place.

Every board should have an annual risk review day when they sit with management and develop a long list of risk that the company may run into and rank them by using a simple formula. Give each identified risk a score out of ten for the probability of it occurring and multiply that by ten for the impact of consequences if it did occur. It will quickly become apparent which are the major risks as distinct from the minor risks that perhaps management can deal with.

The next step is to work out what steps the board can take to mitigate or reduce the chance of these risks occurring. You might think that that is an unsophisticated process but I have found it at least focuses the directors on all the risks at any given time. The monthly board meetings also allow you to identify new risks that have emerged since the annual review date and to discuss the various steps taken to reduce or mitigate risks. These may include a board decision to stop a certain activity as it is too risky or to implement a new policy that management and staff or suppliers must follow to try to minimise any risk.

In a good company, management will undertake its

own risk management process at an operational level and the board may be interested in hearing about the progress on these from time to time. Don't only consider the obvious risks that we can all think of straight away, but also consider opportunity risks that can damage to the company by not taking advantage of opportunities down the track. Some companies may operate in a very risky industry and it's likely the board has requested management to engage external risk consultants to review the company's operations and provide recommendations for implementation.

A board should also consider a more global view of the environment in which the company operates and consider all risks, especially political or economic events, which could impact on the company. Finance is an obvious area to consider, but equally important in my view is occupational health and safety. In some states directors are personally liable for any fatalities or injury suffered by employees even though they were not personally aware of the events that caused it. The severe penalties for directors in these states should help focus your mind on OH&S.

The board should consider what kind of reports it wants in respect to workplace health and safety and ask questions regarding steps taken to try to reduce or eliminate such events. Again, some companies may be in an industry that requires external consultants to provide recommendations to improve workplace health and safety for all its employees.

I have been a director of companies that have unfortunately experienced employee fatalities and in all these cases it was because a staff member's own negligence resulting from ignoring the company's policies and rules. That does not take away from the fact the board feels very deeply for that employee's family and workmates when such an event occurs, whoever has been at fault. Look for innovative ways to continue to drive the safety message from the board through the company by means of staff newsletters and regular toolbox talks from management to staff.

In companies where I have been the chairman, I have asked to be allowed to include an article in the regular staff newsletter to inform staff of any major corporate decisions that the board is able to disclose from time to time, but I have always included a safety message.

There is a hidden danger in any event that could damage the company's reputation. Try to identify risks that may affect the company's credibility as these are not always as obvious as the easily identified hazard or financial risks. The media can make a company's reputation but it can also very quickly break it depending on the events that have occurred.

You should also check how strong your relationships are with your suppliers as any break in the supply chain can be detrimental to your company's ability to produce your goods or services.

Another area to monitor is industrial relations. The board should ensure that it complies with relevant legislation or employment arrangements that have been negotiated.

I have found it's useful to conduct an annual staff survey to find out what employees really think about the company and thus see if there are any emerging issues that will become a risk. It is also useful perhaps once a year to undertake a customer survey to see if there are any trends emerging regarding client dissatisfaction that could become a problem. While you might regard these as operational matters, I think it's useful for a board to at least ask to see the results of these types of surveys. There is nothing wrong with the board inviting key managers or staff to attend the board meeting from time to time in the company of the CEO to get their view on any risks relative to their area of operation and to gain general feedback from the coalface.

The other area of risk management is that of compliance. This means that the board must ensure that the company complies with all the legislation relative to it at federal, state and local government level. Without becoming a lawyer, it's useful for each member of the board to have a broad understanding of a range of legislation relative to the company to understand what is required to meet compliance obligations. This may include the following types of legislation, although it's not an exhaustive list:

- Environment law

- OH&S law

- Taxation law

- Trade practice law

- Employment law

- Corporations law

- Accounting standards

- Any other legislation specific to that company.

Apart from ensuring compliance with the law, it is useful for a board to be able to monitor compliance with its obligations to meet deadlines in respect of various payments or renewal dates to ensure that these are in place. I have found it useful to establish a compliance checklist as part of the board papers which allows directors a very quick way of ensuring compliance with these types of obligations. They may include, for example, due dates for payment of:

- All Commonwealth taxes including GST

- State payroll tax

- Superannuation payments

- Company annual review date

- Lodgement of annual accounts

- Renewal of any required licence

- Renewal dates for all insurance policies held by the company

- Any other due dates for compliance obligations in the company's affairs.

While this is ultimately the responsibility of the CEO, it will often be work of the company secretary of the financial controller to ensure these compliance requirements are met.

This simple checklist helps the board to minimise the risk that the company has not met any compliance requirements at any time.

In summary, risk management is one of the key functions of a board of directors and you should actively seek discussion on this topic at every board meeting and contribute relevant ideas or opinions where you can. If you are acting with care and diligence, then you should be aware of emerging risks and ensure that the minutes record the steps taken by the board to minimise such risks as far as possible.

The reality is that businesses operate in a competitive

commercial world and there will be times when the board has to knowingly take certain commercial risks.

This is acceptable as long as the board has considered all the information before approving any decision to proceed. Any submissions made by the CEO that require board approval should also provide a full analysis of the risks attached to any submission as part of the board's consideration in making its decision. Your due diligence before joining a board should investigate how the board makes decisions and whether they are thorough in considering significant matters and that your opinion will be considered as part of that process.

Don't be afraid of voting against or recording your objection to any decision if you believe the risks are too great. At the end of the day you have to decide what is in the best interests of the shareholders or members. Recent class actions by shareholders against their own directors indicate they won't be happy if you get it wrong.

Chapter 8
Strategy

Earlier in this book I listed what I regard as the key functions for a board of directors. Included in that list was strategy. This means a board needs to spend time looking at the future of the company and reviewing the past. Too many boards spend far too much time considering last month's results and too little on their key function of strategic planning. Looking at the future is not easy, even for experienced directors, but you can develop certain skills and processes to help you contribute to board discussions about the strategic direction of the company for which you are responsible.

Many textbooks and courses are available to help you can study strategy. As I've suggested regarding several other topics covered in this book you should seek out experienced directors and ask them how they go about their strategic thinking and the way they try to make a contribution to the board's role in this area. You're not being effective if all you do at board meetings is ask numerous questions about last month's results and make no contribution for discussions about the company's future.

There are a few basic requirements that a board should include in its annual calendar of activities. These are apart from the fact that strategy should be a permanent agenda item for all board meetings. A board should be involved in the development of a review of any strategic plan together with management, who will probably have done most of the preparation for it. At some stage a board needs to develop some broad guidelines to allow management to understand its thinking regarding any limits or new horizons that it wants it to explore and consider.

I am a great believer in the board and management meeting together for one or two days to hammer all this out and reach final agreement. I stress, however, that it is ultimately the board's responsibility finally to approve or sign off on any strategic plan for the company. This does not mean you rubber stamp what management has given you, nor does it mean that the plan is one entirely written by the board without any management input.

This 'blue sky' strategic planning time should occur early in the calendar year. The CEO then has a clear direction for developing the required business plan for the next financial year and ultimately for developing a draft budget for approval by the end of the current financial year and in time for the financial year about to start.

In preparing for this think tank, the board should give some guidance to management regarding its overall thinking and suggest any research or information the board would like to see as part of strategic consideration.

Some guidance from the board regarding the format for this planning activity is also useful. How many from the senior management team should attend is up to the CEO and the board together. To ensure discussions cover all aspects of the company's operations the CEO should have sounded out his team well beforehand to get their thoughts about future directions in order to bring them to the workshop with the board.

Further research should be gathered in relation to

external factors that may impact the business, such as legislative or political trends, and global and local economic forecasts, particularly in relation to their industry. Any budget preparation should focus solely on profit forecasts but also include capital expenditure requiring approval in the following financial year. This will detail the investment the board is expected to approve by way of capital expenditure to implement any agreed strategic plan.

When I participated in these meetings I always liked to adopt the approach of starting with a clean sheet of paper. In other words, don't take the way the company has operated in the past and extend this into the future, but consider the possibility of almost starting again if that is the best approach. Anything and everything are up for grabs in this free-ranging discussion so that possibilities for innovation, creativity and preparedness for the future are all well thought out.

I have used a number of models as part of my strategic thinking deliberations around a board table. These have included consideration of the key drivers in the company and the core issues that can make or break the business in the future. I have also applied some simple tests to any strategic ideas that are put up for approval. I ask myself the following:

- Is this feasible?

- It is achievable?

- Is it sustainable?

- Who is accountable?

Another simple way to think about strategic thinking is to ask yourself:

- Where are we now?

- Where do we want to get to?

- How are we going to go there?

- What's going to stop us?

- What risks are involved?

The first thing a board has to decide is what timeframe they wish to consider. Most companies tend to have a strategic plan that rolls out between three to five years ahead. Some boards will look to a shorter term and others longer. In my view, anything much longer than five years is probably scenario planning as there are too many unknowns and variables beyond that many years.

It's useful to have an independent facilitator run any strategic planning workshop involving the board and senior management rather than having someone from within the company. A good facilitator will tease out extended thinking and challenge ideas to bring reality to the final outcomes.

All decisions need to be documented in a detailed strategic plan that can be then considered further by the board before finally being approved for management to implement. Given that a strategic plan is an overarching process over a number of years with some long-term goals, it the allows the CEO to produce business plans for each future year and then develop budgets for each plan for the board to consider. In other words, any draft budget should not be considered in isolation from the following year but as part of the financial process towards longer-term goals. All that needs to be considered by the board along with such details as profit objectives for working capital and future dividend policy and balance sheet and cash flow management.

The next thing I suggest a board should consider is adopting a strategy tracker as part of its agenda. This way the board can monitor each month the progress towards achieving steps in the long-term goals in the strategic plan. Too often I have seen very well-prepared strategic plans develop dust in the cupboard while the board merrily counts the paperclips from last month. A tracker can be developed by management to identify each year the key milestones or deadlines that are part of achieving the agreed longer-term goals.

In reviewing this topic, the board can discuss with the CEO the actual implementation of the required steps in the plan. It has been said that most companies fail at the execution stage of the strategic plan and not at the development stage of the plan itself. For this reason, the board needs to monitor the way the CEO is implementing the board's wishes in terms of long-term strategic objectives and the investment of capital by a certain time to fund the plan.

If the board is honest with itself, it should be sure that the plan is being followed step by step along the way. Any strategic plan is there to achieve results for the shareholders or members and to ensure long-term sustainability for the company with minimum risk. A strategic plan provides some framework for the board of management to work with when new opportunities pop up out of the blue.

This way the board can consider whether any such new opportunities fit within the strategic framework and quickly reject them if they don't. I've seen so many boards with well-developed strategic plans suddenly agree to take the company in a completely different direction because a new idea or submission has been put to them out of the blue. That has resulted in failure. That does not mean the board should not consider new opportunities that arise unexpectedly but rather that it should consider these within the general thrust of the strategic direction of the company.

This strategic planning session is an annual event and it may be the board already has a five-year plan in place. This means that it is simply an annual review of the progress in the five-year plan but now extends the five years by a further year into the future taking into account any changes that have occurred in the environment in which the company operates.

I have already suggested that strategy should be a permanent agenda item for every board meeting. However, it's important not to leave this item until the end of the agenda as the meeting may start to run out of time and it receives scant attention at the end of a busy day spent reviewing how many paperclips we used last month.

One board that I chaired agreed to put strategy as the very first agenda item once we had confirmed the minutes and discussed any business arising from the previous month. This meant the directors were still fresh and alert and had no time pressure to consider future company issues. By devoting in the first twenty-five per cent of our board meeting to this topic resulted in enormous changes in the company's growth and profitability in later years.

The types of issues that can be discussed under the strategy topic on the agenda could include the following suggestions:

- A review of the progress on the current strategic plan using the tracker.

- A review of changed circumstances either within the company or external to it that may impact on the current strategic plan.

- Consideration of new opportunities.

- Inviting an outside speaker to attend the board meeting to discuss a topic of strategic interest in their area of expertise.

- Asking a director at the previous meeting to load a discussion based on their research on a particular strategic topic of interest to the company.

- A discussion on any new risks that have emerged that may impact the ability to achieve your desired strategic outcomes.

There is no doubt that to be effective as a director in relation to the strategic discussion around the table, you must be well informed and up to date on current trends. I made it a habit to read the business pages of the daily newspaper as well as listening and watching other media comments. This allowed me to be broadly aware of global and local issues that may have some affect the company. Apart from this, you should be always seeking specific information regarding trends or issues in the industry in which the company operates as well as trends appearing over the horizon.

Having said all that, it's probably likely that the CEO and senior management are closer than you to the coalface if you are a non-executive director. So it's good to have a cup of coffee from time to time to see what they are hearing or observing regarding emerging issues. Talking to other directors in the other industries or business colleagues generally is always useful in gathering information into the computer between your ears for future retrieval when considering strategic matters.

It may help if the board starts to agree on some lead indicators across a range of factors that may affect the company so that you can see trends emerging. It's too late to be looking at lag indicators that tell your company is out of step with the changes occurring around it.

Attending business functions with speakers on a range of topics is also a good source of information to get you thinking and perhaps to share with the rest of your board. Perhaps the company is a member of an industry association or business group that provides research and information to you as well.

The only constant is change. In today's fast-moving and complex global economy change happens at a pace that can catch you off guard if you are not careful. I've seen too many companies where the board has been slow to respond to the changes occurring around them and then find that their competitors have gone past them. Perhaps you will ask why a company does things a certain way. If the response is because that is the way they have always done things then you and the company have a problem.

The minimum legal age to be a director in Australia is eighteen but the average age of company directors is probably fifty to sixty years. The problem with people of that age group tends to be the danger of thinking something should be done a certain way and change should not happen based on your experience. Of whatever age, a director has to be open minded enough to be prepared to see new ways of doing things or to make changes for the company to survive. On the other hand, be careful if you appoint a new CEO who wants to throw the baby out with the bathwater and take the company in a completely different direction so they can make their stamp on the company before they leave.

Strategic planning is a joint effort between the board and senior management, with the board having the final approval on the plans to go forward. To be an effective company director you need to develop the ability to spend time between board meetings considering all the information you gather and reflect on it in relation to any impact on the company's future. A good test is to ask yourself in five years, have a I made a contribution to a board that as a group has made a real difference to the company from where it was five years ago?

Any board that simply minds the store and maintains the status quo is not doing its job. A group of directors must continue to challenge and discuss ways to provide even better outcomes for the company's owner, whether they be shareholders or members. I am sure you can recall, like me, several companies that no longer exist because they failed to move with the times. Your role is to make sure that your company is not one of them tomorrow. In some ways, this is the most enjoyable part of the job of a company director as it really gets you involved in leading the company forward to an even more exciting future and being part of the discussion as to how to you can do it.

As part of any due diligence before joining a board, ask to see a copy of its strategic plan and that will tell you a great deal about how much emphasis the board puts on this part of its role and whether you are happy to be part of that way of doing things.

Very few are natural strategic thinkers and if you have no previous board experience, I suggest you do need to take courses and read widely to try to develop tools and processes to use in your role. No board will appreciate a director who criticises the fact that last month's paperclip usage was up four per cent but contributes nothing to discussions regarding the company's strategic future.

Chapter 9
The CEO

Unless a company is run entirely by executive directors who work in the business full time, it is likely that a board will have a CEO to implement board directions. This chapter is about the person the board chooses to take on that role.

The title may vary. Some companies will appoint a managing director. This person is still the chief executive but also happens to be a member of the board with voting rights. Other companies may appoint a person called a general manager or some similar title. This person is still the senior executive but is not a member of the board. It does not mean, however, they will not attend board meetings to report to the board and answer questions. They will not have a vote.

In some not-for-profit organisations, the chief

executive may have the title of executive director. That does not mean they are actually a director of the organisation, but that they are the senior executive directing the entity on behalf of the board. As a generic title, I prefer to call this person the chief executive officer, or CEO. The principles I focus on in this chapter are the same whatever the title or structure of your company

In the list I provided in an earlier chapter regarding the role of a board, I mentioned one of the functions is appointing and overseeing the CEO. The board recruits and selects a CEO and then manages and monitors their performance. It also is responsible for terminating the CEO's services when they are no longer suitable or required by the company. The constitution of most companies will give the board the authority to do this.

If the board is primarily made up of non-executive directors, it will need a person to run the company on a day-to-day basis. Where I have seen dysfunctional corporate governance is in when the CEO really runs the company and the board don't have much say or control. Shareholders and members elect the directors to provide supervision and guidance of the company on their behalf and the CEO should be accountable to the board to follow these guidelines.

Another problem occurs when there is a complete lack of trust and respect between the board and the CEO, and both sides play games to upset the other while the company falls down around their ears. Then there are the issues created when boards retain a CEO much longer than they should. I encountered one company that had had the same CEO for twenty-eight years and it was obvious that the company's fortunes were slowly declining. Just as a board needs to be continually refreshed and renewed, the CEO also needs to be changed after an appropriate time. How long that is will depend on the company's changing circumstances.

If you are on a board that needs to appoint the company's first ever CEO or perhaps find a replacement for a CEO who has handed in their notice, then the work starts for the board. What the board needs is to ensure it has a clear understanding of what the CEO's role is to be and to have a detailed job description prepared and legal advice obtained regarding an appropriate employment contract. It then needs to consider where the company is at and where it's going and what kind of person it needs to run the company over the next few years. You may find that it's a completely different type of person from the CEO you've had up until now as the company's current circumstances require a different kind of leadership and thinking.

Once this is agreed the board can develop a person specification to go with the job description so that you know the kind of person you want to do the kind of job you now need to be done. The next part of this process is deciding the remuneration. If the board has a remuneration committee, it will be able to provide recommendations to the full board based on external advice and research into an appropriate remuneration package to attract the best candidate.

There has been much media coverage in recent years regarding the large salaries and bonuses paid to CEOs and so the board needs to be sensitive to shareholders' concerns regarding a remuneration that provides incentives and rewards based on actual results achieved. Wherever possible the remuneration arrangements should align the CEO's interests with that of the company and its shareholders. Public companies are now required to obtain shareholder approval for the remuneration policies they adopt for directors and senior officers of the company although it is not a binding vote.

Where companies have not performed, there has been an increasing trend for shareholders to reject such remuneration proposals and ask the board to reconsider. You need to develop a remuneration package that will attract a good candidate and provide some incentive for them to achieve the required outcomes and enable you retain their services for as long as you need them. There is considerable data available to directors these days regarding remuneration matters, including advice on salary packages based on current market conditions provided by external consultants in this field.

I always find it useful to read the annual reports of public companies which provide detailed information regarding remuneration policies and their salary and bonus levels for the top executives.

At this stage the board needs also to decide the process it will use to recruit the new CEO. It may choose to use external head-hunters to find a short list of candidates to be interviewed by the entire board. Alternatively, it may appoint a temporary subcommittee of directors whose job it will be to interview the short list candidates and provide a recommendation for the full board's consideration. Many boards already have a nomination committee in place whose job it is to do this work when required.

In my experience it's better to have a small team of two or three directors, including the chairman, given responsibility for the interviews and final recommendation to the full board. It can be intimidating for a CEO to be interviewed by a large board at the same time and it can result in the possibility of not being able to reach agreement because of the wide range of views.

Using an external recruitment agency or head-hunter is probably a good investment regardless of what it costs. Trying to save dollars and have a board run its own advertising and search can be lengthy and inefficient. It may be that time is something you don't have as the current CEO has already left or is seeing out their notice to leave the board with nobody in place except perhaps an acting CEO from within the existing management team. On that note, a board has a responsibility to develop a succession plan so that other senior managers are being groomed ready for promotion to the CEO role at some future point.

This assumes the board believes that promotion from within is the best step whereas other boards may prefer to bring an outside person into the senior team. Note, however, that I have seen quite often when a board chooses the latter method, that the company then loses senior executives who feel they were not given the opportunity despite years of valuable contributions to the company.

Given that a board is not there to run the company on a day-to-day basis, it's critical that you get it right in choosing the CEO you want. While you may have time constraints, you don't want to be rushed into picking anyone for the sake of filling the role as a wrong decision can be disastrous. It may be that the board has lost confidence in its current CEO but is prepared to let them stay without them realising that the board is already searching for their replacement ready in time for their departure. The board's ability to achieve this kind of well-planned transition only occurs if they're active in monitoring the performance of a CEO on a regular basis.

*   *   *

This leads me to the next important function for the board in relation to the CEO, which is having a robust performance review program in place.

Again the board needs to decide the process it will use for this. It may be simply the chairman who meets with the CEO to provide feedback based on the collective thoughts of fellow directors. Or it may be a small subcommittee of the board including the chairman that provides this review feedback as part of an annual calendar of events. Any CEO should be reviewed at the end of an agreed probationary period after appointment and then at least once a year on a formal basis as well as with one or two other informal reviews throughout the year if required.

The board can only monitor the CEO's performance against the already agreed job description and key performance indicators set out within their employment contract. Care is needed to ensure you don't create a legal minefield for the board and company by terminating a CEO for vague reasons that are not specific to the performance indicators. I have seen boards that try to remove CEOs because they simply did not like the person, even though they were achieving all the outcomes required.

A problem I have seen with some boards is that several of the directors have been CEOs of other organisations or, even worse, the former CEO of the same company, and tend to form a judgement based on how they think the job should be done. That is indefensible. If the CEO achieves the desired outcomes the board is seeking, but has done it in a way or in a style that is different to yours, then does it really matter?

There is no argument about a board terminating a CEO for other obvious issues such as fraud or misconduct or any other breach of their employment contract. If a board chooses to remove a CEO based on a statement that 'they have lost confidence in them,' I suggest you need to obtain legal advice to be very sure of your grounds, despite how you may feel. There needs to be clear evidence as to why the board has lost confidence in this person and there will probably be few difficulties if the facts would lead any other reasonable person to draw the same conclusions.

* * *

It's important for the CEO to be reminded well ahead that a performance review is coming up, perhaps in a month or a date already agreed to, and to invite them to prepare for the review.

At the same time, all the directors should give some thought to the CEO's performance and contribute to an agreed board position to be shared with the person at that review. Keep in mind that it's a two-way process in which the CEO should be given the opportunity to express their views about the company and the board, and raise any concerns for consideration by the directors.

It should be an opportunity for the board to express recognition of the positive things the CEO has achieved, as well as raising the areas it believes require improvement or changes. At the end, there should be documented and agreed outcomes for action in relation to the CEO's activities in the year ahead.

I have never been much of a believer in linking salary reviews to performance reviews at the same time as it can create an expectation that it's simply time for the annual remuneration review. However, many boards will complete the performance review and then go back and consider the remuneration package for any changes or increases based on outcomes of that review. If you are happy with the CEO and would like them to stay, the board should consider any changes in remuneration trends in the marketplace in order to remain competitive as part of that salary review.

It's also a good opportunity to reconsider any performance incentives to make sure they're still in line with company's needs and the person's expectations in a competitive market. The board's role is to appoint the right CEO and get rid of the wrong CEO, monitoring their performance while they remain in the role.

*   *   *

At this point I need to raise the issue of established protocols. I have seen dysfunctional corporate governance occur when there are blurred lines between the role of the board and that of the CEO and senior management. One example is when directors approach staff without the CEO's knowledge and instruct them to undertake certain actions or seek information of a sensitive nature. Another example would be to have the CEO or senior management provide information to some directors and not others as part of the game they wish to play.

It is important for the board to understand it is not there to run the company on a day-to-day basis (unless the board consists entirely of executive directors). Remember the adage that there is no sense in getting a dog and then trying to do the barking yourself. If you believe you've picked the right person and they have a clear set of goals, the board should stay out of the kitchen and let the person get on with the job.

Don't spend time at board meetings trying to give advice to the CEO about how you would do things or criticise them for the way they're doing them.

Also respect the fact this person will generally have the authority to hire the managers and staff that they choose and the day belongs to the CEO and not the board. Exceptions may be where a board wishes to be involved in the final selection of a chief financial officer or company secretary but not others.

For these reasons it's useful to establish some documented protocols to avoid these kinds of issues. These vary from company to company but may include guidelines on some of the following possible scenarios:

- Confirming the process a director should follow before approaching any staff member that works for the CEO. This may include the simply courtesy of advising the CEO first before approaching the staff member and ensuring that the director does not give any instructions to that staff member.

- A process to follow if management or staff wish to approach an individual director with some concerns or sensitive information. The solution here may be to have it approved by the CEO first and then passed through the chairman to the appropriate director. In most cases the chairman can be the gatekeeper for the board and the CEO can be the gatekeeper for the management and staff.

Such protocols should also include defining what information can be passed around or provided within the company and perhaps protocols regarding invitations to various company functions or activities. Once these rules are agreed, they should be documented and circulated so that the board and all staff understand the processes to be used within the dynamics of the company.

Quite often in non-profit organisations I've found that well-meaning volunteer directors want to try to contribute even more than being a director. This has resulted in them turning up day after day trying to tell staff members what to do and interfering in ways that create a mess for the CEO to clean up. I've also seen considerable discord created when staff members have contacted directors after hours to pass on gossip or other issues. On that note, good companies have a whistle-blower policy that allows people to report activities or issues that are of concern. This does not mean the board may not be the ultimate recipient of whistle-blower information if the CEO is the person is causing the problem of concern to the whistle-blower.

This is pretty rare but I have had a staff member contact me after hours to report some unsavoury activity by the CEO, of which the board was unaware. The person felt they had nowhere else to go to try to resolve the threats being made by the CEO in respect to these matters. The board acted quickly once we gained firm evidence of the allegations, which resulted in the immediate dismissal of the CEO. I noticed our action had an amazing positive effect on staff morale.

It's important that trust exists between the board and the CEO, with everyone pulling in the same direction for the good of the company. This is particularly true in the relationship between the chairman and the CEO, who will meet more regularly than the other directors. This provides the opportunity for the chairman to give informal feedback on the

CEO's performance and listen on an informal basis to any concerns the CEO has. When we talk about the chairman's role later in this book you will see there is a responsibility to be a mentor and sounding board for the CEO as chairman of the company. This means that the CEO feels confident in discussing any issue with the chairman and seeking their counsel on personal or business matters of concern to them as CEO.

I have found quite often that a CEO is happy to make a decision but simply wants to bounce options off me as the chairman to get my opinion. Quite often they've decided to move with an option different from the one I've suggested, but they have at least taken the opportunity to get an objective opinion on their choices.

It doesn't matter how good a board is if it has the wrong CEO as the board will not achieve its objectives on behalf of shareholders or members. It's important for a board to choose the right person for the company's future, give them some clear guidelines and directions, and then let them get on with the job.

Reward them appropriately but not excessively and know when it's time to get a different person at the helm. The CEO should expect absolute support and trust from the board, and any board will expect the same in return from the CEO.

If you get a combination right, it can make a huge difference. A good board and CEO working together can produce amazing results. A company I chaired selected a CEO who improved the profitability of the company tenfold in five years, expanded the company nationally in the same period and attracted some of the best talent in the industry to key positions. On the other hand, I read the case of a board that appointed a CEO who decided to ignore the board's strategic plan and set off in another direction, the result being that the company made its first loss in fifty years at the end of his first year in the job.

On another issue, I read recently that the number of female CEOs of public listed companies in Australia can be counted on one hand. I don't think the number is much bigger for private companies. This is disappointing and I believe that boards, which are still unfortunately male dominated, have not accepted that female CEOs can be equally as valuable as their male counterparts. I have met some incredibly talented women around board tables and in senior management positions, both within government and the private sector and more particularly in the not-for-profit sector. Every director should try to encourage an increase in these numbers for the good of everyone.

Finally, unless you are the sole director of your own business where you are working every day, I repeat the advice I gave to you as a company director: stay out of the kitchen.

Chapter 10
The Chairman

S o you want to be a company director? It's probably also true that you would like one day to be a chairman of a board as well. I can only share with you that I have learnt that being a chairman is a more complex role than simply being a member of a board as a director.

There is no doubt that a chairman can make or break the effectiveness of a board of directors. You may have already seen yourself many cases of committees or boards led by people whose only contribution is to make the whole group dysfunctional. This is because they dominate all the discussion and resist any objection or criticism of the way they want things done.

Equally, I've seen chairman who provide no leadership or direction and allow board or committee meetings to turn into an absolute rabble with nothing decided.

Somewhere in between is the person who is respected by their fellow directors and puts extra time and effort in to making sure the board functions well.

They must strike the balance between encouraging everyone's contribution and opinions to be heard, while being firm in managing the discussion so that is reaches outcomes or decisions within a reasonable time frame. Again, there are numerous books and courses available on how to be a chairman. Google produces plenty of research and writings which may help you understand how to fill this role.

It's interesting that the Corporations Act simply states that the chairman is the person who chairs the meeting. Therefore they do not appear to have any power or authority beyond that of other directors although recent law cases in Australia seem to imply there may be a higher degree of liability as a result of the person holding this office. That debate is for another day.

While the chairman has no extra formal authority, they can however provide firm leadership by gaining the respect of their fellow directors and avoiding some of the bad examples I outlined earlier. A chairman will generally be paid at one-and-a-half to two times the level of fees of the other directors because the workload will generally be this much greater. The marketplace seems to indicate that a deputy chairman will be paid about 1.2 times that of the other directors. This is to recognise they may have to stand in for the chairman from time to time, but otherwise have no greater workload than the rest of the board.

The chairman is usually an ex officio member of any board committees, meaning they could attend all of them if they wish. The chairman also must liaise regularly with the company secretary and the CEO as outlined in the previous chapter. They will also be the figurehead that attends major company functions and represents the company together with the CEO. It may be board policy that it is the chairman rather than the CEO who speaks to the media on any company matters.

The chairman may also be expected to confirm the agenda for forthcoming board meetings and ensure all board papers are ready to be sent out with sufficient notice before the meeting. All this is on top of their need as a director to keep abreast of all the research, information and briefings undertaken by any other director, while also making time to meet external advisors to the board such as the auditors.

Some chairmen are appointed directly by the vote of the shareholders or members, while others are chosen from the directors appointed by the owners. Generally, they will already have had experience on the board as a director, but some companies appoint their chairman from outside the current board, depending on the circumstances. If you look at public companies, chairmen seem to hold the role for between five and ten years, after which it's probably appropriate to consider a new person for the role as the board continues its succession plan of renewal.

The term chairman is applicable to a male or female person in this role. Or the word chairperson can be used.

I won't say much more in this book about the role of a chairman as it is intended as a guide for those looking to join a board for the first time or with experience only as a director. It is an incredibly satisfying and enjoyable role if you put in the time and work required. Keep in mind the chairman should be the guardian of the standards of the board and this includes leading the process of board performance reviews and providing feedback and counselling to individual directors where required. Equally, they should also continually seek feedback from the board regarding their own performance and be prepared to improve if necessary.

Conducting the annual general meeting of shareholders can be a challenging and interesting time for a chairman. A well-run AGM is evidence of an effective chairman who is doing their job. Working with the company secretary to ensure the annual report and other shareholder communications are completed in a timely manner is also part of the role. Finally, the chairman should be the supervisor of the board's corporate governance standards and processes, and not be afraid to comment when standards need to be improved or maintained by the company's directors and officers.

The chairman plays a pivotal role and requires a set of skills over and above those needed by the other directors. Perhaps one day I'll write a book solely for chairman. But now is not the time nor place for too much detail on that topic.

Chapter 11
Director Dynamics

One thing I've observed over many years on various boards is the behaviour and dynamics of my colleagues around the board table. If you want to be a company director, you will need to understand what happens around you and how it impacts how the board operates. In other words, the decision-making process becomes more complex the more people you have involved.

The constitution of a company will dictate the minimum and maximum number of directors. This can range from a single-shareholder/single-director company up to one not-for-profit organisation I encountered that had twenty-eight people on its board. Historically it is felt that a number of people elected by the owners (shareholders or members) probably produce better decisions and provide a range of experience and skills before making a decision agreed upon by the majority, if not everyone. In some ways, the chairman is like the referee of a football match or conductor of an orchestra who is trying to adjudicate and bring together a wide variety of behaviours and opinions in achieving a common cause or decision.

A director must not be afraid to express their individual views and have the courage of their convictions. However, they must also accept the majority decision and the members of the team who support that decision. This means the director cannot then undermine the board's decisions by continually disagreeing with it in public, otherwise they should probably consider resigning from the board.

Unfortunately, I have seen behaviour over the years that has not been in keeping with this spirit. Not-for-profit boards have often been the worst offenders in seeing volunteer directors go straight to the media, expressing disagreement with decisions made at yesterday's board meeting and undermining the credibility of the organisation. This might be all right if you are a councillor in a local government authority but is not appropriate in a boardroom. Equally, the CEO and other senior officers of the company need to accept the board's decisions and directions and be united in their support of such deliberations.

Here are some examples of the behaviour that is not helpful in a board. You may have observed similar behaviour in other committees or groups you've been involved in.

First, there is the person who dominates the conversation and continually tries to force their view on everyone else. While such people can add value to a board in clearly expressing strongly held views, it's important they allow others to have a chance to express their view, even if it disagrees with their own. Such people often cut across others who are trying to speak and interrupt all the time. They also tend to talk loudly and often appear to be threatening or bullying in their behaviour if they don't get their way.

A good chairman must act quickly to bring this person back to a level of participation acceptable to everybody. However, when it is the chairman who exhibits this kind of dynamic, this creates problems for the rest of the board. When this occurs all the other directors must make it clear to the chairman that they are simply one director among several, even if they are chairing the meeting.

Another type of person is the one who lacks patience. This is often because they are a quick thinker who has reached their own conclusions and their mind is already racing ahead to the next issue. You will see them checking their watch while somebody else speaks, or perhaps tapping their fingers on the table and providing body language that shows they are in hurry to get on with it. A good chairman must remind this person that everybody must be given time to have their say within the confines of the overall time limits.

One problem in being appointed to a board is you don't yet know what skills the others around you possess. It is said you can pick your friends but not your relatives. It is also true that you can't pick your fellow directors once you've accepted a board appointment. If you find others are not like you, you must learn to accept the differences and allow them to participate and make their own contribution to board discussions. An impatient person must train themselves to take the time to listen actively to other people and wait for matters to come to a timely conclusion before moving on to the next agenda item.

Equally, it's not useful as a director if you arrive at a meeting ill prepared and delay proceedings because of lack of preparation. It also means that you don't talk for twenty minutes on a point that could have been made succinctly in five minutes. You don't want to contribute to any lack of efficiency in the board by continuing to debate issues well beyond the point where everybody else has reached a conclusion and is ready to make a decision, even if this decision appears to be going against your point of view.

They will challenge the status quo and question things in a way that others have not thought of. I must admit the reason I can live with this kind of person is because I probably have these same tendencies.

The type of director I find difficult to accept is the one who makes no contribution at all. How often have I seen people sit through an entire board meeting without saying one word during the entire proceedings, reading their board papers and flicking through them to get up to speed while missing any opportunity to contribute to the debate or decisions. Quite often they will vote the way that the majority are leaning without offering any analysis or discussion on the point being decided.

A good chairman has an obligation to try to draw out such people by asking them directly if they have a point of view or if they have any questions they would like to raise before decisions are made. Having done that myself as a chairman I'm still surprised to find such people admit they have nothing to say.

This is not to say that an effective director is not someone who is quiet and reserved for much of the time. Often such people, when they do speak, add enormous value with their quietly spoken but very well-considered points of view or questions that get everybody thinking. I've learnt that when such people do speak, it's well worthwhile listening to them carefully as they usually have something valuable to add.

Another type of person to look out for is one with no original thought of their own. Quite often they will team up with another director and simply follow their voting pattern. Alternatively, they will simply vote the way they were influenced by what was said by the last speaker. This person is adding little value on behalf of the people who appointed them to the board.

A similar type of problem is stems from a director who clearly has no understanding of the matters being discussed, but is not prepared to admit they don't know, or even ask questions to try to find out. I've seen directors sit there with a glazed look in their eyes, clearly out of their depth about any issues with some degree of complexity and then vote the way the majority do. Not only is that fairly dangerous for the individual director not knowing what they have voted for, but again it is unfair to the shareholders or members who put them there.

A good chairman should be aware of this type of problem and have a private discussion with the person to encourage them to undertake further training or study to try to improve their skill level in any areas of weakness.

I started by talking about the director with a dominant personality who tends to try to override everybody else with their point of view. The other person to watch for is the CEO who is equally dominant with a personality that can easily influence people. This may be because they have a strong personality that bears no opposition. Or they may have had some success so far and are wearing an invisible halo that says they can do no wrong and they should not be challenged or questioned.

I've seen in not-for-profit organisations on a number of occasions the result is that the CEO ends up making the decisions while the directors go through the formality of agreeing to those decisions. That's not to say it's true in the case of all not-for-profit entities, but it does appear to be more prolific with this type of organisation rather than with fully commercial profit-making companies.

While there should be respect and trust between the board and the CEO, directors must remember they have the ultimate authority on behalf of the owners to make decisions about a number of issues, while the CEO is left with autonomy to make decisions in their specified area of responsibility.

*   *   *

I am often asked about the role of a managing director versus that of a general manager. I have already explained that the managing director is the CEO but is also a member of the board and has a vote, while the general manager attends the board meetings but has no vote.

I do wonder about the difficulties facing a board

when one of its members is also the person accountable to the board for the implementation of board directives. A smart managing director will always remember that they can be removed by the board while only the owners can remove the directors. Hopefully a good collegiate atmosphere operates so that the MD and the rest of the board work together as a team in a cooperative way.

Another area of concern is the creation of factions or ginger groups within a board of directors. This is not uncommon and human nature often allows this to happen. However, it's not healthy that some directors want to form voting blocs as they should be working together as a team for the good of the owners instead of spending time having private meetings or lobbying the rest of the board for their particular point of view as a subgroup. This is what occurs in politics but I don't believe it has any place within committees or boards and a good chairman needs to address this issue in a frank and open manner if it arises.

On the same note, directors should not allow personal differences to interfere with their professional approach to doing a job as a member of a board. You don't have to necessarily be friends with your fellow directors, but you should at least respect each other, even if you agree to disagree on matters from time to time.

It's often been said that an effective board is one that encourages robust disagreement. This means it is healthy to have opposing points of view on major issues as long as the discussion eventually leads to a decision. I have said before that a good director will keep an independent mind and not be afraid to express their point of view, even if they are the odd one out with the rest of the board. It does not mean, however, that you should be obstructionist in disagreeing with everything for the sake of it. You should be able to quickly read the general mood of the board and see if the majority view is heading in a certain direction and be ready to accept that majority view when the time comes after you've had your opportunity to express your point of view.

I have observed board meetings that have gone on for hours because an individual would not give up fighting for a point of view long after it was clear that they were the only person holding that view and yet would not accept the chairman's ruling on getting a decision and moving to the next item.

Finally, there is the problem of the person who lacks any manners when participating in a board meeting. This is the person who will spend all their time reading board papers or working on their laptop while ignoring the rest of the meeting. This person sends and receives SMS messages or mobile phone calls and talks on their phone during the meeting. They are often the same person that will simply get up and go out of the room to make a phone call or attend to some other matter thus holding up proceedings until they return. A good chairman will develop the intuition to know when it is time for a comfort break before the whole board resumes the meeting and is able to focus on matters at hand.

This can also be the same director who continues private conversations with the person next to them while the rest of the board is trying to debate critical issues. This is not only rude and disruptive, but extremely unprofessional. An effective board will exhibit dynamics that allow robust discussion and timely decisions under the chairman's leadership. Sometimes the most effective decision a board can make is to agree not to make a decision at a particular meeting but to defer it until more information is available. After a few hours people start to get mentally tired and care must be taken not to fall into the trap of going round and round in circles on one issue if they can't reach a conclusion.

A chairman needs to be firm about not allowing continual interruptions from outside the boardroom unless it's a matter of extreme emergency. I've seen staff and other people wandering into meetings on a regular basis to talk to directors, get decisions from the CEO, or have papers signed. I've never found that a few hours on one day a month for a board meeting means the company stops operating while board and management are doing their job.

I will discuss board performance reviews later, but these are opportunities for the directors to have a robust discussion about the dynamics of everyone around the board table. You should be prepared to accept any criticism of your behaviour that does not contribute to effective dynamics for the board.

Chapter 12
Board Papers

A board can only be as effective as the quality of the papers it receives from management. It should spend time discussing what it wants in the way of board papers so that management can meet these requirements. It is not appropriate that a board accepts without question what it is given because it is what management thought it should have.

To meet your legal obligation to act with care and diligence, it's important that you know what you don't know. Otherwise you may find you are overwhelmed with volumes of information that you don't need but do not receive reports on the critical issues that you do need to consider.

In my experience, management generally has always been willing to change the contents of the board reports it provides once it has guidance from the board and understands the reasons for needing this information. Be careful you don't become overwhelmed with large volumes of operational detail that you may not need. The board's role in monitoring the affairs of the company generally will be at a higher corporate level across such areas such as strategy, risk finances, et cetera.

Let's start with the agenda. I've frequently found this has been the weak link in the effectiveness of a board. Often it is because the agenda has been set by the CEO in the absence of any guidance from the chair or board. The agenda should usually contain some standard template headings such as the following:

- Apologies

- Confirming the previous minutes

- Business arising from the previous minute

- CEO report

- Financials

- Strategic tracking

- Risk management

- Compliance checklist

- Capital expenditure submissions

- Other submissions requiring approval

- Other general business

- Date of the next meeting

There should be a deadline for all agenda items and other board papers to be with the company secretary before the board meeting. This allows the compilation of the board papers in a timely manner so they can be sent to all directors at least three or four days before the actual board meeting. This gives the directors time to read the papers and raise any questions offline before the meeting itself. For this reason, most board meetings are held towards the end of each month, thus allowing time for the financials from the previous

147

month to be finalised and for the CEO to write a report based on those financials and prepare the board papers for issue with that amount of notice.

A good chairman will not allow directors to mention twenty-three new topics without any warning because they forgot to put these agenda items in on time. It's not fair for directors to be asked to consider a new topic without any supporting paperwork and no warning and be asked to make decisions on it, although there may be urgent exceptions if the chairman believes they are appropriate and necessary.

Be sure the agenda contains all the appropriate items but is not so lengthy that the board would need four days to get through it. Often the chairman and CEO will discuss the timing of agenda items in order of priority before finalising it.

One suggestion to consider is moving strategy up to be in the early part of the meeting rather than leaving it to the last minute. It's important that a board doesn't spend its whole time simply reviewing what happened last month and not enough time is provided to discuss the future of the company. Too often any strategic discussion has run out of time at the end of meeting when people are tired and it can get lost. Discussing strategy early in the meeting has worked very effectively for boards where directors with a fresh mind have had a meaningful discussion about the strategic direction of the company and spent less time checking up on how many paperclips were used in the past month.

The agenda needs to be an effective tool for ensuring the board considers all the topics necessary with the appropriate level of priority and within a reasonable timeframe. I've met some chairman who have boasted that their meeting takes only an hour each month and I wonder if the board is really on top of what's happening in their company. By contrast, I've seen some board meetings for small to medium-sized companies go all day and even all night and you have to wonder what they spend so long talking about.

Depending on the type of company and the size and complexity of the business, board meeting durations will vary but generally half a day is the average for a typical small to medium or small public unlisted company. A public listed company board meeting make take a full day, while some public companies have opted for meetings less frequent than monthly but extending over two days or more. The only legal requirement is that the board must meet at least once a year to sign off on the annual accounts. Any frequency beyond that is up to the discretion of the board unless it is stipulated in the constitution.

*   *   *

The content of the board papers will vary for each company, but if you look at the agenda listed above, it becomes clear what kind of reports you can probably expect.

First, the report from the CEO should provide some general overview comments on the previous reporting period and action being taken to address any problems or variations that have occurred. The rest of this report may range across several topics including comments on the financial result, as well as functional activities such as human resources, marketing, IT, industrial relations, legal or contractual matters, et cetera. The report may end with any formal submissions the CEO is making for board approval.

The test of a good report from a CEO is that a director can read it and have a good understanding of what's happening in the company even if they cannot attend the meeting. If the report does not give sufficient information, be prepared to ask the CEO at the meeting any questions needed to gather further information or a better understanding on matters the CEO raised.

The financial report will probably follow a format similar to that outlined in the earlier chapter on finances. It's up to the board to decide what financial information they need or don't need and what format it should be in for ease of understanding.

The risk management report will follow a format that the board has decided on which may include a review of the agreed risks and their ranked scores and steps being taken to reduce such risks, together with details of any new risks identified. I've already mentioned a strategic tracker, which I have found to be a useful document in listing the milestones or KPIs that need to be met as part of achieving longer-term strategic goals or objectives.

I found it useful for a board to have a compliance checklist. This is a moving monthly report on a list of matters requiring compliance by the company. This will vary for each company but may include some of the following.

- Taxation payment due dates

- Superannuation payment due dates

- Licence renewal dates

- Insurance policy renewal dates

- Any other statutory reporting deadlines

- Any other compliance requirement

Other reports may cover workplace health and safety or other operational matters of interest to the board together with any legal or contractual documents for consideration.

It is useful for board papers to be bound and perhaps separated with colour divider pages with tabs between each section for ease of access and identification. Having all the board papers numbered from beginning to end also makes it easier for directors to refer to a particular page under discussion without having to flick through all the papers trying to find it. The agenda is usually the first page on the bound document and any other major reports or abnormal documents outside of regular board papers should be kept as separate articles to the main board papers. When reviewing board papers before a meeting it helps to mark key points either with pen or highlighter or perhaps insert question marks or brief notes. Be careful what you write on the board papers as there has been a legal case which rested to a significant extent on comments written by the director in those papers and used as evidence.

Once the minutes have been confirmed by the board at the beginning of the meeting, they should be signed by the chairman and dated with each page initialled and then returned to the company secretary for safekeeping. I have often been asked whether you should keep all your board papers, particularly as your liability extends for seven years after you've left the board, and my answer is 'No.' A company is required by law to keep all such minutes and probably the board papers themselves as an original set which can be obtained through a deed of access. This is provided for under the Corporations Act.

*   *   *

Having already mentioned the approval of the previous meeting's minutes, I should comment more about these.

The first question a board considers is who should take the minutes. Larger companies will have a company secretary with the knowledge and skill to fulfil that role. If they lack that ability, the board should insist on them undertaking some professional training and development to ensure they can do their job on behalf of the board.

Smaller companies often will invite a secretarial person from within the staff to take minutes. I question this practice as it's not always appropriate for a junior staff member to be listening to confidential discussions about the company's affairs with the board hoping they will keep such information private. I have been on boards that have used the services of professional outside contract company secretaries who have the skills and knowledge to advise the board on a range of matters while also taking the minutes in a professional and confidential manner. What is not appropriate is to have the CEO or one of the directors trying to take minutes while also being expected to participate in discussions in a meaningful way.

With the growth of technology it is quite appropriate

for the minute-taking to be put straight into a laptop computer. Other minute-takers prefer to take written notes and finalise these in full form after the meeting. Regardless of which method is used it is important that the draft minutes are sent to the chairman for checking before being issued to all directors within two or three days after the meeting.

This timetable allows directors to check the accuracy of the minutes while the meeting is fresh in their memory. It also gives all parties involved time to act on matters that have been delegated to them with plenty of time before the next board meeting. For this reason, it's good practice to insert people's initials next to each decision so that it's quite clear who has responsibility for implementing it. More times than not, this will be the CEO but sometimes it will be the chairman or an individual director who has been given the task of turning decisions into action.

It is not acceptable at a board meeting to find that a decision requesting action a month ago has not been followed up by a person because they forgot about it or say they haven't had time to do anything about it.

A chairman should keep the momentum moving forward by getting things done, but this does not mean everything has to be done within the following month. Some matters may need months to act upon to ensure they are brought to a conclusion. For this reason, the chairman will often request that a decision from the previous month be rolled over so that there is a continuing record of a matter that has not yet been finalised and that it does not slip through the cracks.

Once a board has confirmed the minutes are a true and accurate record of the previous meeting and are signed by the chairman they cannot be altered in any way. They become the official record of the meeting's proceedings and could be used as evidence in court if required. This is the signed copy that is kept at the company's registered office. Individual copies are sent to directors which they may or may not choose to keep themselves.

In summary, a good board will work out what it wants and does not want in the way of board papers and will review these at least once a year to ensure it allows the directors to be fully informed about the company's affairs. Make sure that your board does not have too little or too much in the way of board papers.

Chapter 13
Committees

A board of directors is allowed to form committees to help it fulfil its role. Such committees may be permanent or ad hoc, formed for a short term for a specific project and then disbanded. Larger and particularly publicly listed companies will always have an appropriate number of board committees while small to medium companies may have only one or two, if any.

If a board does have committees, you can be expected to be appointed to at least one of them and your due diligence before accepting any board appointment might include a discussion with the chairman about which committees you'll be asked to join.

To confirm my earlier statement, a committee should have no decision-making ability but provide an opportunity to consider a particular area of company's operations in more depth and then make recommendations to the full board for a final decision. It's dangerous to be a member of board that meets each month only to find that significant decisions have been made by a small number of directors sitting as a committee and all directors are now legally bound to that decision.

This is why I am not in favour of executive committees that boards sometimes use. These tend to consist of the chairman and one or two other directors who have the authority to make decisions on significant issues in between board meetings without involving all the directors. Urgent matters between meetings can be easily dealt with by way of circulating resolutions (flying minutes) which allow all the directors to have ownership of the decision. Don't forget to ratify such flying minutes at the subsequent board meeting and have this recorded in the minutes.

Another mistake I've seen some boards make is to form committees that deal with functional areas of the business that really should be left to management. These, for example, might include human resources, IT, marketing, or production and supply. This is not the role of the board and you simply end up with a second layer of management and a board that is not focusing on the key issues that are its responsibility.

If we go back to the role of the board that I defined earlier in this book, we see that its responsibilities include the following:

- Strategy,

- Risk management,

- Policy making,

- Monitoring, and

- Selecting and monitoring the CEO.

This may provide a guide to the type of committees a board will form. For example, you may choose to have a strategy committee that explores external trends to provide ongoing input to the board's strategic thinking. You may choose to create a risk management committee to focus on this topic for board consideration.

Another committee that may or may not be appropriate

to your board is a corporate governance committee. This group will monitor compliance issues as well as the development of new corporate polices at a board level and general corporate governance standards.

An obvious potential committee is one dealing with finance. This is not to mean such a group looks after financial matters entirely as that is the responsibility of the entire board. However, it can undertake some of the more in-depth work on financial matters and make recommendations to the board.

Those companies that require an annual audit of finances will probably have an audit function looked at on a more regular basis on its behalf, while receiving reports and recommendations about this key area of the company's function. Some companies have combined audit, risk management and compliance into one committee as there is some synergy between these three matters.

Boards of larger companies will often have a nomination committee to continually look at the succession plans for the CEO and other senior management as well as searching for candidates for any board vacancies.

Publicly listed companies will inevitably have a

remuneration committee. In recent years there has been a stronger spotlight on remuneration policies and the levels of fees paid to directors and senior executives in companies where shareholders have a non-binding vote on the remuneration policy at the AGM. This committee will continually monitor market level remuneration for directors and officers, together with recommendations for policy development in order to attract and retain the best talent while meeting shareholder expectations.

I said earlier that the board may consider establishing an ad hoc committee with a sunset clause whose task is to look at a particular function or project over a limited period and make recommendations to the board. For this reason, the board needs to continually look at all issues affecting the company and detect any areas needing more time and work than the board can provide. It will delegate the workload in this specific area to a subcommittee, thus leaving the board free to focus on major ongoing issues.

It's important for the board to choose the right people to be on any committees it creates so that you have the best level of skills and input. The board is entitled to co-opt outside people who are not directors to a committee. For example, any finance or audit committee that does not include an accountant is probably not as fully capable as it should be in discharging its duties.

From time to time a board may consider including management or staff on a committee if they have skills or knowledge that will assist that committee's deliberations. In most cases the board chairman is an ex-officio member of all committees and may attend any committee meeting. It's also useful to be sure that the person appointed to the chair of a committee has the skills to lead it effectively in doing its job on behalf of the board.

Generally, a board should establish a calendar for the coming twelve months, listing the significant events throughout the year, starting with the board meetings themselves. Such a calendar should include dates for all committee meetings throughout the year.

Note that it's not effective to have committee meetings the night before a board meeting as it allows insufficient time for the preparation of any documented recommendations for consideration by the board. While this may be the only time you have all the directors, including the committee members, together is one place that is not sufficient reason to try to jam them close together. Most committees meet two to three times a year, depending on their function. These should be spread out with sufficient time between them and the board meetings.

While the board can delegate authority, it can never delegate responsibility. Ultimately it must have ownership of the outcomes of any committee deliberations and recommendations and this needs to be made clear to the committee. For this reason, it's especially important that the committee has a clearly defined job description about what its function is and what authority is delegated to it. But this does not include the authority to make decisions that bind the whole board.

I've observed committees spending a lot of time discussing matters that were not relevant to what they were set up to do and spending no time at all considering issues they were supposed to be dealing with. Make sure there is clarity about the committee's function and that it is understood by all that committee's members.

If management or staff are invited to participate in any board committees, it's important the committee chair is firm enough to ensure it is not taken over by management or staff and that the directors have the final say on what recommendations are submitted to the board. The effectiveness of the whole board committee process will break down if management or staff end up having too much control or say in the committee's work. There is no doubt that their expertise and knowledge are useful as part of committee discussions, but directors need to consider it from a wider corporate perspective on behalf of the company's owners.

In the previous chapter I mentioned the possible content of board papers but did not include committee reports. If your board does have committees, it should have a section in the board papers for individual committee reports, including an executive summary of recommendations with clear resolutions for the board to decide.

Finally, it's useful for a board to have a spring cleaning and review its current committee structure. Boards can find they have committees that are obsolete and no longer required, while at the same time they may lack committees needed because of changed circumstances within the company.

In publicly listed companies, directors are paid committee fees over and above their main board fees, while management and staff participating in such committees will be paid their normal salary with this included as part of their job. Any outside experts seconded to board committees will need to be paid relevant professional fees.

Some boards have a policy of not paying extra fees for committee work. This is something the board should consider and seek external advice regarding appropriate committee fees.

Chapter 14
Board Meetings

have touched on this topic in other parts of this book, but I thought it useful to dedicate a chapter to it for additional consideration.

I have alluded to the way the duration of board meetings can vary depending on the type and size of the company. When asked how long a board meeting should last, my answer is generally, 'As long as it takes for the board to do its job and no longer.' In other words, don't rush through short meetings because everyone's too busy, but don't have excruciatingly long meetings because people waffle on about topics completely irrelevant to the agenda.

Many years ago I was asked to join a board which was to meet at 9am. This was not a large company by any means. The chairman asked me what kind of pizza I liked. When I asked why he wanted to know, he explained the board always had pizza sent in for the evening meal.

I have also indicated elsewhere that a good chairman is like an orchestra conductor. They must know how to move though the agenda in a timely manner while allowing everybody an opportunity to say what they think. You must be prepared to express your point of view without fear or favour and be prepared to ask the questions you need to fully understand the issues you're being asked to vote on. However, it also means that if the majority of directors decides for a different option, you will need to accept this as the majority view and allow the meeting to move on.

As a well-known country and western singer once said, 'You have to know when to hold them and know when to fold them.' You have the legal right to be heard at a board meeting as a legally appointed director and you should not let any chairman try to shut you down unless you are continuing to fight a losing battle on a decision you have already lost.

I also mentioned the need for a board calendar. Any good board will agree on having a calendar for the coming twelve months listing major events affecting the board. These include the board meetings and committee meetings and perhaps other special meetings such as strategic planning or risk review, as well as its own board performance review.

There may be other events in the calendar such as the lodgement dates for annual accounts or other deadlines to be met plus any other company functions or activities. These may include trips by the board to the company's operations within Australia or overseas as these are a useful exercise for any board whenever they are possible.

It's important for directors to receive board approval to be absent from a meeting but note the constitution may provide for the removal of a director in the event of non-attendance at more than three or four meetings.

It's important that the board spends time considering a wide range of areas and does not fall into the trap of simply looking at last month's results. There have been some well-developed academic models about effective boards that indicate the balance of time best spent by a board on several topics. These functional areas would probably include time spent on the following:

- Internal monitoring,

- External reporting,

- Performance management,

- Strategic planning

In other words, a board needs to spend time looking at the past as well as the future, providing oversights as well as foresights.

The review of the previous month's result should focus on things that are exceptional to the norm for discussion rather than going through every line item in fine detail with no time left for the other functional areas listed above.

I have already alluded to minimising interruptions to board meetings so that you do not have directors wandering in and out of the room or staff coming in and out seeking the CEO's attention. This means it's best you ask directors to switch off mobile phones and private laptops during the meeting to prevent phones ringing in the boardroom unnecessarily. At the same time check if your current venue is appropriate for an effective meeting. If not, look for an alternative venue which may be away from the company's premises.

Think about at what time of the day you want to have your meetings and, where possible, try to have them start in the morning while participants' minds are still fresh, rather than late in the day when people can start to become mentally tired. I've sat through board meetings for hours with no breakfast or comfort stops or tea and coffee breaks, let alone anything to eat. It's hard for directors to remain focused if they are not given a pit stop or they are starving and thirsty. Jugs of water on the table are useful and adequate lighting and minimal external noise or other distractions are recommended too.

The Corporations Act states that if the appointed chairman has not arrived within fifteen minutes of the starting time given in the notice of meeting, the directors are able to appoint another person to chair the meeting. There is nothing worse than intense discussions being interrupted by the late arrival of some directors because of their own tardiness.

As I said at the start of the book, it is useful to sit back, listen and observe when attending your first board meeting. This will equip you with much useful information in terms of the way the board operates and the dynamics of the individuals around the table.

Before accepting the board appointment ask the chairman if you can sit through a board meeting before making a decision. This avoids the risk of joining a board only to find its meetings are a complete circus. If you have an ineffective chairman who has no control of the meeting, you and other directors have an obligation to provide robust feedback to that person.

Bear in mind my earlier suggestion that boards include in their annual calendar meetings away from the regular venue and near other locations relevant to the company's operations. Not only does this give the directors an opportunity to see the company's operations in other locations and meet some of the staff in those places, but it indicates to the staff and other stakeholders the board's interest is away from head office. I find it also provides an opportunity for further bonding between the board members as they travel to such locations and attend any social events that may be organised around the board meeting itself. It also creates excellent public relations opportunities for the company by way of media articles and press statements in that local area.

Finally, your board performance reviews, which I discuss in the next chapter, should consider at least once a year how effective your meetings are and what you can do to improve them. Always keep in mind that you are a director 365 days a year and the meetings are only the tip of the iceberg in doing a job. Directors are paid to think about the company between board meetings as well as during them.

Chapter 15
Board Performance

I t has always been my view that boards of directors should conduct a performance review on themselves in much the same way as they expect to do on the CEO who, in turn, they expect to conduct performance reviews on the staff.

I once read an exceptionally good book about corporate governance entitled, *The Fish Rots from the Head* by Bob Garratt (Profile Books, published 2011, and Amazon), which shows that companies with problems often find the trouble starts right at the top through poor performance from the directors.

As part of your due diligence before joining a board, you should ask the chairman if they conduct board performance reviews and, if they do, how frequently and what methods are used. If the response is that they don't do any such thing, you might ask the chairman if they are prepared to consider starting such a process if you join the board. If it is not interested in doing this, you would have to question how seriously the board takes itself in relation to its own performance.

One of the problems that I have observed is that too often the board takes the credit for the company's year end result and thinks it is doing an excellent job. The reality may be that the company has a particularly good CEO, management team and staff who produce the results despite what may be a dysfunctional board. While it's important for the board to monitor the company's result as well as the performance of the CEO, it's equally important for the board to monitor its own performance without attaching to much significance to the company's results each year.

As I mentioned earlier, it's not a bad idea for the board to invite a different director each month to conduct a five-minute review of the board meeting just after it's finished. Over twelve months this gives every director a chance to observe the board meeting while being part of it in preparation for the five-minute review. The chairman should encourage the director doing such a mini review to be frank and honest in their comments regarding what has happened. This person can then comment on the quality of the board papers as well as the dynamics of the meeting and its agenda. They can also provide some diplomatic feedback to the chairman or other directors regarding things that that director has observed as well as commenting on their own performance. With some boards it is the chairman who does the five-minute review but the danger here is that they may not necessarily comment on their own performance as the chair.

From surveys that I have read over many years there has been a definite increase in the number of boards conducting performance reviews on themselves. From memory, only ten years ago fewer than five per cent of boards undertook such an exercise, whereas the most recent figures indicate that nearly half the boards surveyed undertake some kind of performance review. This is a pleasing trend and is possibly in response to shareholders' demands.

There are several methods a board can use to undertake such a review with the frequency at the discretion of the board. Most boards do it at least annually, while others extend it to a biannual event or even less frequently. Fewer boards appear to conduct them two or three times a year but it may be a little too much to undertake a full review that often.

The first basic decision a board has to make concerns methodology. It can decide to review itself or engage an external consultant to undertake the review. Apart from the obvious cost, the advantage of the latter is it allows for an independent and objective view using a more rigorous methodology and process together with a more detailed report and recommendations. As part of the information gathering the consultant may offer to sit through a board meeting and take note as an observer and to review a typical set of board papers and minutes.

A consultant is then able to write up a report highlighting the areas that require improvement, together with recommendations on how to do this. If a board uses this external process, it is important it makes sure it follows up the recommended actions for improvement so that meaningful changes actually occur.

If you use the same consultant for each review, they will keep records of the results from previous reviews and be able to compare any changes in the key areas identified at the next review. There are several corporate governance consultants who can provide this service.

The more common practice at the moment appears to be for boards to undertake reviews themselves without external help. Here, too, the board has several methods to choose from and it should discuss the most appropriate method before doing the review. One choice for the chairman to open discussion at the end of a board meeting on the review date and to invite all directors to contribute their thoughts regarding the period under review. It may or may not invite the CEO or company secretary to join the discussion to provide their input from a different perspective. It will become apparent following the discussion and suggestions from the board what they can do to improve in these areas.

Another method is for the chair to conduct a private interview with individual directors. This allows them to provide feedback regarding that person's performance as observed by the chair and to invite feedback from each director on the chair's own performance.

Another possibility is to use some of the tools that a consultant would use. These include inviting the directors to complete questionnaires or provide written comments to be summarised by the chair, who can then provide a verbal or written summary to the board without naming individuals making the comments.

Whichever method a board uses, the process needs to be conducted in a professional manner so that directors do not feel threatened but rather see it as a useful exercise for the good of the whole board and the company.

The next question is to decide what you should review if you accept my proposition that the company's actual results are only one part of the total equation. For the board as a whole, areas to look at would include whether:

- The agenda has been appropriate for the company and its meetings.

- The quality of board papers and reports has been appropriate.

- The quality of the minutes has been accurate and appropriate.

- Attendance of directors has been sufficient at all meetings.

- The board has worked as a cohesive team with little friction or disharmony.

- Individual directors have been allowed to be frank and forthright in their opinions.

- The chair has effectively controlled the meetings and provided leadership.

- The relationship between the board and the CEO has been healthy.

- Board activities throughout the year have covered the key functional areas outlined earlier in this book, e.g. strategy, risk, policy, monitoring, CEO performance, et cetera.

- The board has been able to react quickly to any crisis or major event in the company's life.

- Shareholders appear to be satisfied with the board and the company's performance.

- Annual reports and other milestone events have been met.

- The AGM has been conducted effectively.

- All board committees have made a useful contribution.

- The company secretary has been effective in their role.

You can see the many factors a board can consider in reviewing its own performance, and further discussion will no doubt generate other topics to be considered. If your company holds an annual general meeting that shareholders attend, that also acts as a kind of annual report card or feedback for the directors apart from the formal review process that undertaken.

One thing you must always consider is your own performance as a member of any board. Rather than wait for any formal board performance review, I have always found it useful to sit back from time to time and consider my performance on a particular board. If you take the job seriously, your own professional standards will force you to ensure that you are making an effective and useful contribution throughout the year. A formal review will give you some feedback, whether it be through a consultant's report or from the chairman direct, but that's always after the event.

It is better to seek informal feedback more regularly throughout the year. If you are a new director, there is nothing wrong with asking the chairman to have a cup of coffee every few months and invite their comments regarding your performance. If you feel comfortable in talking to one or two other members of the board, you may seek their feedback from time to time as well. Too often I've seen directors who have simply been taking up space on a board and adding no value whatsoever or who do it on a voluntary basis. You should always keep an eye on the way you are operating as a member of the board.

Think about some of types of behaviour I described in the chapter on director dynamics and make sure you are not conducting yourself poorly. Questions you can ask yourself from time to time could include:

- Do I miss many board meetings or other company activities?

- Do I attend meetings without having read the board papers?

- Do I vote on issues that I don't really understand?

- Do I contribute to the discussions around the table?

- Do I offer new ideas or suggestions for board consideration?

- Have I undertaken further professional development in the past year?

- Do I have a better understanding of the industry this company is in than I did twelve months ago?

- Do I have a good professional relationship with my fellow directors and the CEO?

- Have I spent any time thinking about the company and its future outside of board meetings?

Again you can see there are several topics you can

consider privately and you may think of others to review from time to time.

One question I think a board should ask itself at least once a year is whether the company is better off than it was a year ago because of the board's input. You can ask yourself much the same question every twelve months: have I made a contribution to the board and the company that has added value?

In my experience, one has to guard against potential complacency the longer one stays on any board. I've often seen the dynamics of a board that has been together for a long time where they all agree to agree on everything. Watch out for any tendency to have unwritten rules that nobody challenges anything that might upset 'the club.' This is one good reason a board should continually renew itself though a change of chair or directors.

On that note, a board should have a documented succession plan. It will generally have one for the CEO and other key officers and should have one for itself. While most directors are appointed for an average term of three years, some can be up for re-election annually at the AGM. Despite this, it's not uncommon for directors to remain on the same board for five to ten years or even longer. This is why a good board will have a nomination committee continually looking for potential candidates and knowing a timetable that has to be met for finding replacements over a medium-term cycle.

A good chairman or director should also know themselves when they have reached their use-by date and indicate that they will not be offering themselves for re-election at some point in the future. We have all seen politicians who don't know when to quit and who have overstayed their welcome with the voters. You don't want that to happen with your shareholders.

Don't be afraid of board performance reviews. They are valuable exercises in ensuring continuous improvement for a high achieving board. All directors should ensure that the fish does not rot from the head.

Finally, an important process in board performance is the need for directors to undertake regular professional development. The only people I have met who actually do know it all are teenagers. Mature adults should consider life as a continuous learning experience and welcome the opportunity to gain knowledge. A good board will often have a program for the coming twelve months mapped out for professional development for all its members with funds allocated in the budget for such activities.

Of course, there will be times when you will need to put your hand in your own pocket to pay for personal training or education; you should regard this is an investment in yourself.

Now, let's talk more about professional development

. . .

Chapter 16
Professional Development

f you accept my argument that we're never too old to learn, then you should be looking for ways to further your knowledge in your role as a company director. There is a range of public courses available, particularly those offered by the AICD. You can start with some of the half-day modules on a range of topics then progress to attending the complete company directors' course.

Some years ago I completed the advanced company directors' diploma and found it to be a different experiential exercise from the original course, which was conducted in the traditional lecturing manner. For those directors on international boards, the AICD also offers a course tailored to their particular needs.

If you think I am giving the AICD a big plug, you

would be perfectly correct. I find it fascinating that the only requirement to be a company director in Australia is to be over eighteen years of age. In my view, at least the basic company directors' course should be a qualification to make you eligible to join boards, particularly public ones.

Outside the obvious formal courses, there are numerous other resources offering professional development in areas in which you might like to be better at than you are now. For example, many professional member bodies in management or accounting provide short courses on aspects of financial management.

There is even a professional member organisation for company secretaries which directors can join. It not only offers courses specific to that role, but also useful courses in a wider range of corporate governance topics.

I have often been asked what skills or knowledge a company director needs and have frequently surprised people with my answer. They expect me to say a person in this role must be strong in finance or in production or in marketing or human resources for example. These are functional roles best left to management, but if you do have knowledge in such areas, it's bonus for the board. Too often I've seen lawyers or accountants on boards who have been expected to be providing free in-house advice to the board rather than using external professional advisors.

Instead, a director should have broad knowledge across most areas of a business and then undertake further studies to strengthen the areas in which they're weakest. The most important skill in my view is the ability to be an independent thinker and able to absorb large amounts of information and analyse them. In many ways, a good director simply needs to use common sense, which is not always common. So the kind of professional development you may consider are those I've outlined already in this chapter that include corporate governance and the significant areas of any business generally.

*   *   *

Apart from courses, there are several other ways today to gain learning.

I have found Google to be one of the best tools for directors. You can research just about anything on your computer and access all manner of information and knowledge. And the good thing is that you can do this 24/7 in the comfort of your own home or your office.

In addition to online resources, there is a huge range of books available on the many topics of interest to a director. Most bookstores carry a selection of books on business, including topics such as corporate governance or finance or strategy. If you can't find a book in store you can generally buy them online after doing a search.

*   *   *

Apart from this kind of professional development, you need to continually further your knowledge of the industry in which your company operates. The initial induction to the board should have given you basic information about the company and its industry. Wherever possible you should be seeking more knowledge by attending any conferences, seminars, trade shows and the like that are relative to your company and its industry. Seeking further updates and briefings from the CEO and senior management is also useful as is talking to staff as you meet them in your role.

When joining a board, I have always tried to learn sufficient to enable me to answer questions about the key drivers that will make or break the company.

Talking to directors who have been on the board much longer than you is a useful way to get their perspective on the company and its industry as well as its management and staff. Another way to obtain a better understanding of the industry is to look for publicly available annual reports on competitor companies or undertake desktop research from time to time about emerging trends or issues in the industry. You should be continually abreast of global and national issues that can impact your company. These can include the economic situation as well the political scenario, demographic or market changes. I have found it useful for boards to conduct an employee survey at least once a year as well as a customer survey via management to get a handle on what both these groups are thinking.

Finally, over many years I have found it immensely helpful to develop the habit of keeping up to date with the latest news. Reading the newspapers every day and subscribing to relevant magazines or watching certain television programs can provide interesting information that is part of the thinking mix in your role as a director. You should keep an eye out for any information or new ideas that are emerging that you can ask about at the next board meeting to see if they could be relevant for your company.

I have seen boards that have failed to allow the company to be current and have watched their competitors pass them by and markets disappear.

It is always useful to ask yourself what is it that you don't know and then try to find the answers. This active self-learning is a necessary part of your role in meeting your obligations to the shareholders or members. If you don't understand the terminology or technology that your CEO and staff are using, then you need to learn. Directors will often be on company boards in an industry in which they've had no previous experience. This places a greater obligation on them to get up to speed as quickly as possible about that industry so they can make a meaningful contribution. If they don't or won't, then don't be afraid to invest in yourself.

I always found it useful to seek out mentors in the form of other experienced directors or chairmen and thus gain from their wisdom and experience as part of my professional development.

CHAPTER 17
FAMILY COMPANIES

As it says in the title of Paul Kelly's song From Little Things Big Things Grow, many family companies have grown from small beginnings to become large and successful businesses. Often they reach a point where the founders see the need for a proper board with outside directors. In this role you are a mentor as well as a board member.

I have had great pleasure contributing to family companies as a non-executive chairman or director. However, they bring challenges not found in non-family companies and these are what I will explain in this chapter.

Your due diligence should extend to investigating the family situation and any personalities or issues that will hinder a good board. Be aware of any 'protected species' in the business or a dominant founder who is used to getting their way.

If the board's processes and meetings are not well established, you may need to establish these to ensure they are not management meetings in disguise.

Under their constitution some family companies

may have a governing director. As part of your due diligence check if the constitution allows for such a position. These are not so common today but often existed in family companies in years gone by. This position was usually held by the founder of the company or its main shareholder or owner who wanted to retain final control despite having other members on the board.

A governing director has the right of final veto over any board decision and this can negate the value of having other family members or external directors on the board if this power is exercised too frequently. I was once invited to join the board of a family-owned company with a governing director as the first independent or external non-executive director in the company's history. To the credit of the governing director, they never exercised this right of final veto at any time during my time on the board. I was, however, always aware of their thinking and generally tried to accommodate their views unless it was not in the best interests of the company or the other shareholders.

There is a reasonable amount of truth in the old saying that you don't mix business and family. While it has worked well for a number of family-owned companies on occasions it has also created a dysfunctional board and a fair amount of tension within the family as a result. I have seen cases where the father, who may have been the company's founder, tell his children they were now to be directors alongside him only to find they had no real say. Another problem that can often occur is that younger members of the family have insufficient skills to be a company director.

The law has several cases that makes it clear that ignorance is no defence.

For this reason, I have never been keen on the idea of family members being appointed to boards to make up the numbers. I have met many family members who have been directors and yet never attended a board meeting or ever seen any board papers or reports. Family squabbles have resulted of such appointments. This is a generalised statement as I've also seen many successful family-run companies with all members of the board actively contributing to good governance.

A further problem can exist where all the directors work in the business on a day-to-day basis. Too often the result of this is a lack of attention to their responsibilities as directors as distinct from their role as an employee and problems can occur. The first problem is the lack of attention to compliance and good governance thus creating a lack of objectivity or strategic thinking. In other words, one has to be careful that the directors don't work *in* the business instead of *on* the business. For all these reasons, family directors need to set up the discipline of holding regular board meetings with minutes kept and board papers prepared as distinct from operational or management meetings.

Founding directors should ask, 'Are these family members we wish to appoint to the board the best people to be directors of our company?' If you are a family member and are invited to join the board of the family company, you should ask yourself, 'Do I have the skills and time to devote to my role as a director, as distinct from being a family member or employee of the company?'

This is the reason directors of family-owned companies reach a point where they realise they will benefit from recruiting an external non-executive director to their family board. This may be because of a decision to prepare the company for a listing on the Stock Exchange or perhaps prepare it for a potential trade sale. It can be a recognition that the company has outgrown the skill level of family directors and now needs to develop the systems and processes of a larger business.

It could be that the founding directors are getting on in years and have no younger family members willing or able to join the family board and so wish to prepare the company for a transition to a board of non-family members for the future.

I recall being asked to join the board of a family-owned business where the founding director who was the father had appointed his two adult sons and all their wives to the board even though the women had nothing at all to do with the company. Following a family feud, one son and wife left the business and the town while the other said he had no long-term view in the business. It was at that point the father appointed non-executive directors to prepare the company over the next three years ready for eventual sale, which we did.

If you are invited to be the first outside director on a family board, you need to do your homework very carefully before accepting. Will you find the family always sticking together to out-vote you, even if the direction they're heading in is the wrong one in your opinion?

Will they listen to your advice or suggestions and will the board meetings turn into personality clashes and family squabbles?

Will the founding director insist on remaining as the chair of the board even if they have no skills in running board meetings?

If none of these are issues, then by all means accept any offer to join the board and look forward to making a contribution.

You also might check if the founding director has appointed family members to key management positions and whether they are un-sackable or promoted way beyond their ability. In other words, be sure when joining a family board as an outside director that the family is prepared to accept change in respect to some of these issues in order to achieve proper governance outside of any family factors. At the end of the day, your job is to contribute to board decisions that continue to grow the company and its wealth for the shareholders in the family.

While being sensitive to the family relationships and personalities, you cannot act any differently from if you were on any other more public board without these influences. You will still need to ask the hard questions and express your views robustly and discharge your legal duties to the shareholders. Be careful not to fall in the trap of being expected to make decisions that favour one group of shareholders in the extended family to the detriment of other family members who may also be shareholders. Never forget that you must act at all times in the interests of all shareholders and not only some. You may find there are factions or ginger groups within the extended family of shareholders that could create tensions for you as well.

In my experience on family-owned boards, the other directors have always been keen to learn and are looking to you for advice and guidance in formalising governance processes within the company. This can be extremely satisfying and offers you the opportunity to make a real mark on that company by sharing your skills and knowledge with other directors with lesser experience.

You may find family members who work in the business and who are directors are not paid any additional fees for their board role as distinct from their executive role. This can sometimes lead to an expectation that your board appointment will be for extremely low fees, if any at all. You need to explain to these shareholders that you are being appointed to a professional role and have no other benefit as a member of the family or as a shareholder. It also means you have accepted the liability that goes with such a role as well as the extra time and effort you will be asked to contribute that you would not find in a non-family company board.

Don't be surprised to find they have no directors' and officers' liability insurance and may not have even heard of it. Before joining the board you must insist that the company takes out such a policy not only for your own sake, but also for the benefit of the other family directors.

If the family-owned board feels it is now ready to appoint outsiders to the board, I would usually recommend they consider appointing that person as the chairman with the necessary skills for that role. It also means there is a referee or umpire at the board table with no hidden family agendas driving their decisions when guiding the board. It can be very frustrating being a director on a board where the founder is still the chairman with no ability to run board meetings and the habit of still wanting everything their way.

A smaller family company could feel they cannot afford to pay a director's fees at the level that the market requires. They may offer you shares in the company in lieu of fees. If it's a newly established or start-up company, that can be a risk as the shares may not pay dividends for a long time and you could find that you have worked for nothing. Accepting professional fees and no other benefit allows you to remain truly independent, which is a quality they will value in time.

Having said all that, joining a family board can be a very satisfying and interesting role. Not only will your input be welcome in most cases, but you can get to be part of an exciting business in an interesting industry with particularly good prospects. Once you understand the shareholders' intentions for the long-term future of the company you have a clear track to make a meaningful contribution around the board table.

In my experience, such family companies usually include excellent people who are a pleasure to know. In some cases, I have made friends with such businesspeople and remained so long after I have left the board. Not only do you get to know about an industry or business that you may have had no exposure to previously, but they also get to learn a lot from you if you're doing the job properly.

While you may officially be a director, you will often find you are also an advisor and confidante to the other directors and indeed some of the family shareholders. Don't always expect that you'll be meeting in a well-fitted-out boardroom or that the company secretary or minutes taker has all the skills you will find in a public company. You will, however, usually be offered an excellent morning tea and lunch. It doesn't really matter if your board meeting is around the kitchen table, as long as the directors focus on matters a board should discuss and meetings are not allowed to become too operational.

Don't assume a family-owned company necessarily implies that it's small. I've been involved with family-owned companies with hundreds of employees and turnover that is greater than some publicly listed companies. Your best contribution as an external director is to make sure the board keeps a focus on the future in respect of such things as succession planning and exit strategies for family members and shareholders.

Earlier in the book I distinguished between small and large proprietary companies and you should keep an eye on the thresholds that I listed to see if the company moves into the category of a large private company with subsequent additional obligations. I recall joining a board of a family company that grew very rapidly and moved from being a small to a large proprietary company. I was the first non-family director. At the end of the first year I had the pleasure of seeing the shareholders receive their very first dividend in the twenty-year history of the company. As they said to me, 'How long has this been going on?'

If you are a founder of a family business, don't always assume your children will have the necessary interest or skills to lead the business after you retire. History shows many companies are sold or wound up by the time the third generation gains control for many of the reasons I have already set out. If you are a family member or outside director being asked to join the board, make sure you clarify the several issues outlined earlier.

Family companies are in their thousands in Australia and some say are the backbone of our economy. They employ thousands of people and contribute significantly to the economy. Being a director of such a company can be terrific opportunity if the circumstances are right.

Chapter 18
Not-For-Profits

I would be remiss of me to end this book without talking about not-for-profit boards. There is something like 700,000 not-for-profit entities in Australia and they make a significant contribution to the economy. Yet in most cases the directors are volunteers who give their time freely. Unfortunately, the corporate governance standards in years gone by has not been as good as it could be, although this is improving rapidly.

Let me clarify what not-for-profit means. I have met board members from such organisations who thought the entity was not allowed to make any profit at all. This meant they either minimised income or maximised expense near the end of the financial year to try to achieve a zero figure.

The reality is that all not-for-profits are expected to

make a profit (usually called a surplus). But they are not allowed to distribute these profits back to the members or owners in the way that for-profit companies do for their shareholders. Instead, any profit or surplus must be reinvested back in the entity for the benefit of its members and its causes. Logically the board should focus on making a profit so it has more to reinvest in achieving its objectives as a not-for-profit entity and creating financial sustainability for the future.

Broadly speaking, not-for-profit entities fall into two main types of corporate structure, although there are some other legal versions, but these are in the minority.

First, a company limited by guarantee is an entity regulated by ASIC and subject to the Corporations Act like any other company. It has a board of directors and is owned by the members of that entity. As the name implies, the debts of the company in the event of its winding up are guaranteed by members. The good news is that this is limited to a nominal amount for each member as set out in the constitution and it could, for example, be only $10 or $20 each. The directors have unlimited liability, as do the directors of any other company, in relation to the debts of the company. Such a company can operate anywhere in

Australia and is not limited by any state or territory boundaries.

An incorporated association is created within a particular Australian state or territory. It generally can operate only within that state or territory, although in some circumstances it can apply for permission to operate outside those borders. These entities are regulated by a state government department (e.g. the Office of Fair Trading) and instead of a board of directors, has a management committee. Its constitution is usually based on model rules and the penalties for committee members are nowhere near as severe as for company directors. The reason for this is to not discourage members of the community wishing to volunteer their time on such committees but at the same time providing a small level of penalties should they breach the relevant Incorporation Associations Act. Such a committee must consist of a president, secretary and treasurer as well as other committee members. Note that the board of a company limited by guarantee usually has a chairman only and the rest are simply other members of the board, although they also require a company secretary.

Regardless of the type of entity they are,

not-for-profits operate across a wide range of activities within the community doing good work for others. Such not-for-profit entities can extend to your local sporting clubs or other activities of common interest to members as well as large licensed clubs such as an RSL. Quite often not-for-profit entities will be given tax concessions or exemptions depending on what they do and receive federal or state government grants to assist in meeting their objectives. Apart from legislation specific to companies or incorporated associations, they may also be subject to a range of other legislation relevant to their particular operation. For example, private schools are usually not-for-profit entities but are subject to the appropriate education legislation by their very nature.

More often than not the size of the board or management committee is larger in number than that for a commercial business seeking to make a profit. This may be because it is keen to attract as many 'helpers' as possible around the board table or they have simply kept adding more people over the years. Sometimes they can become dysfunctional purely because of their sheer size.

I mentioned early in this book that being invited to join a not-for-profit board is a good way of gaining experience as a director with a view to eventually being paid board fees for a commercial company directorship. However, you need to be sure that you spend your time on the board of a not-for-profit company in a field that genuinely interests you and in which you want to help. In other words, you must have a real interest in the objectives of that entity and in what it does and see it as a way of making a useful contribution while also learning about boards.

It's important that you do your due diligence thoroughly before accepting any offer to join a not-for-profit board. In my experience it's more often the case than not that you will see poor corporate governance practices and become part of a dysfunctional board, and that can become frustrating. A board may consist of people with a personal agenda and are there for the prestige of being associated with this particular not-for-profit. Others may have a genuine passion for the objectives of the not-for-profit but have no skill for being a director. Good intentions, no matter how honourable, do not replace skill and experience around a board table.

You may be expected to help fundraise or get involved in operational activities as a volunteer with little time or emphasis on the board function. It could be that the CEO (who may be the only person being paid) has real control of the entity and the directors go along with whatever they are told. This may be because they feel they don't understand the issues as well as the CEO and bow to a more dominant personality when making critical decisions.

Sometimes directors are appointed to not-for-profit boards as a representative from an organisation that has some vested interest in the business. They may be a government appointee or a representative from some other governing entities related to that sport or charity, et cetera. Often people are picked on a geographic basis to give a voice to more remote regions without any consideration about their ability to be a member of the board. You may find some directors don't respect the confidentiality of board meetings and last night's decisions are today's gossip or public news due to a clash of personalities or other longstanding issues based on the history of the organisation.

For any of these reasons you need to consider very carefully before saying yes to joining a not-for-profit board. If, however, you are satisfied that none of the issues exist then by all means look forward to joining the board and making a useful contribution. Make sure the chair is a person with a firm nature and able to control meetings so that they don't turn into an operational squabble or go on for hours and hours while they debate the colour of the balloons for the next fundraising function.

While most not-for-profits are legally required to be audited, you still need to keep a close eye on the finances to minimise the risk of fraud or insolvency. A recent report claimed that fraud was being committed in more charities than in commercial businesses in the past ten years. A lack of control or a general view that everybody can be trusted can be dangerous for any not-for-profit. You should ask for and expect sufficient board papers and minutes with appropriate reports to allow you to be fully informed from a governance point of view.

If the board or committee is dysfunctional, the other danger is that the organisation will eventually lose a talented CEO and other key staff. They become frustrated with the clear lack of direction or leadership from the board or the continuing politics and tensions. I have had CEOs of not-for-profits tell me of stories of well-meaning directors or committee members being in the office every day interfering in the running of the organisation because they 'just wanted to help.' At the same time, these directors were ignoring their board responsibilities, usually through lack of knowledge or interest.

* * *

Having said all that, there are many successful not-for-profit entities in Australia and New Zealand with highly effective boards that have guided the organisation over many years. There has been an emerging trend over the last few years for not-for-profits to pay fees to board members, even if it is only nominal amount. I strongly support this trend and believe it can change a director's understanding of their responsibilities. It helps remove the volunteer mentality that allows board members to turn up only when they feel like it and take an active interest if they have any spare time. Once a person is paid by that organisation, it should create a sense of obligation to do the job properly.

Recognising that some directors on not-for-profit boards come with good intentions but not the necessary skills has resulted in further professional development. Good not-for-profits now budget a modest amount to fund the training and development of their board members. They see this as an investment in the organisation itself. Such entities recognise that a good board can make a huge difference to the success of the organisation now and in the future. As a director of a not-for-profit entity your focus first and foremost is on running the business and not on devoting your time to the good work the organisation does.

As one CEO said to me, 'No business equals no mission.' If the board does not ensure the organisation continues to exist and operate in a business-like manner, it may not survive to continue achieving its mission in the community. Usually the organisation will have engaged professional staff to help the not-for-profit achieve its objectives and this should not be left to the board. The board should try to adopt the same practices and processes as used by a larger commercial board to ensure good governance within the limits of the entity's resources.

Don't always assume, however, that a not-for-profit has limited resources. I have seen some organisations with staff numbers and turnover larger than some public companies. Make sure you are not recruited to a not-for-profit board because you have particular skills or qualifications. Too often such boards recruit people with experience in marketing, human resources, IT, fundraising or law or accounting. They then think they will be getting professional advice in a consulting capacity at no cost while ignoring the fact that you are there as a director with a wider interest than your specific expertise.

*　　*　　*

Changing the topic for a moment, I'd like to talk about government boards. While these are not strictly not-for-profit, many of them are not involved in operations that have the prime purpose of making a profit to distribute to shareholders.

Such entities can be established at a federal or state government level or by a local council. They usually pay directors' fees although generally at less than the market levels for fully commercial private sector companies. Some people are keen to be invited to join government boards as they see prestige in having their name associated with such organisation. I have never understood why they think this as in a lot of cases they can be more complex and politically sensitive than commercial boards.

Some government-owned corporations are set up to provide a service to the public while also making a profit. This results in the payment of a dividend to the government as the owner. Sometimes the board will be told by the shareholding minister how much the dividend will be so that the matter is taken completely out of its hands. The shareholding minister will often exercise the right to remove board members and appoint new ones and this will often occur after a change of government following an election. I have seen cases where the shareholding minister instructs the chief executive and bypasses the board and does not even inform the board of their decisions.

If the government entity is not established to make a profit but simply to provide a community service, the board will be judged on the standard of that government-provided service, rather than the financial results. In such cases, it becomes a not-for-profit organisation as any surplus will be deemed to be reinvested to provide an even better community service rather than any dividend distribution.

Some government entities also set up advisory boards, which may be paid or unpaid, where community citizens are asked to provide expertise or advice but have no decision-making power or authority. This can be an interesting role to take on as long as you know that the government entity or minister has not established this to appear to be consultative and will ignore everything you do.

The other problem that can exist with government boards is that their commercial decisions can be influenced by political considerations not encountered in the private sector. It may also open up the opportunity to have your name in the media as a result of the position you hold on that board. So, while government boards are not strictly not-for-profit entities, I see a lot of similarities and they deserve a mention in this chapter.

I am not entirely critical or negative about not-for-profit boards; it's just that they can be more challenging and demanding than commercial boards. I have enjoyed participation in not-for-profit boards and have gained great satisfaction from knowing that I have made a contribution to an organisation that has really achieved its community objectives and helped a lot of people.

Apart from the fact that you will usually be giving up your time on weekends or weeknights to attend not-for-profit board meetings, your skills and experience as a director are usually welcomed by not-for-profit boards. If the organisation operates in field of activity really close to your heart, then you have the added bonus of knowing you have done good work for others in your community as well as for the board itself.

There are many professional development courses and books available devoted to not-for-profit boards. These are usually well-run courses and well-written books and all add to the increasing professionalism of not-for-profit boards everywhere. If you think you have the time and skill to make a commitment to a not-for-profit board, I hope you enjoy it as much as I have.

Chapter 19
Getting Off

As I began this book by talking about how to become a member of a board, it seems only fitting that I should conclude by telling you how to step down from such a role.

There may be many reasons you wish to quit. You may feel you have been there too long and it's time to make way for new people. Perhaps you have become frustrated with a dysfunctional board and you realise there is nothing more you can do or contribute. It could be that you are concerned that the company is becoming financially riskier despite your objections or concern. Or it may simply be that you no longer have the time or the availability to remain on a board and in fairness you need to leave.

Another reason for leaving a board may be because

others have decided you should go. This could be that the shareholders do not choose to re-elect you at in an annual general meeting, for example. In a smaller company it may be that the majority of shareholders wish to appoint other directors and have asked you to resign. Also a smaller company may decide it cannot afford to continue paying all the directors, or perhaps there has been a change of ownership and the new owners wish to appoint their own people.

I mentioned earlier that the shareholders appoint the directors, but they can also dis-appoint the directors. This small play on words means that they have the right to remove you at any time, even if your letter of appointment indicates a certain period or term for that appointment. It is not an employment contract and shareholders can exercise their right for a variety of reasons.

Assuming it is your decision to leave, you must consider the questions of resignation very carefully. If the situation in the company has become so impossible that you cannot continue, that is understandable. However, it means that you are walking out on the shareholders you have been appointed to protect and resigning may not be the best thing you can do for them. Naturally, you will resign when the board becomes completely dysfunctional and you are unable to save it from itself. Equally, if the other directors continually out-vote you on most issues, you probably have no future on that board.

I have always held the view that until the situation becomes completely impossible, you owe the shareholders or members the obligation to stay and continue the fight from inside the tent rather than outside. Even though a board cannot remove a director, you will often find there is considerable pressure from other board members to make your life uncomfortable if they wish to do so. Generally, if a chairman taps you on the shoulder and says the other directors have no confidence in you any longer, it may be prudent to offer your resignation. If, however, you believe this is simply politics and a power play is in force to gain their own way, then you might decide to dig your heels in and stay.

Whatever the reason for your decision to resign you need to go through a certain process to do so. On a public company board, you simply indicate that you will not be available for re-election at the AGM and your tenure will cease at that time. If you decide to resign from a board midterm because of ill health or other reasons mentioned earlier, then you need to do the following:

- Write a letter of resignation to the company secretary with a copy for the chairman.

- State a date on which you wish to cease being a director and ensure that your resignation covers any other subsidiary companies with which you are involved.

- As a courtesy, you should meet with the chairman to indicate your intention to resign and if possible, also let your fellow directors know.

- In your letter to the company secretary, ask them to complete the necessary forms and submit these with a copy of your letter of resignation to ASIC to be effective from the date that you have indicated.

- Make it a practice to pay for a search of ASIC records a few weeks later to ensure it has processed your resignation as you legally remain a director until ASIC records your cessation on its database.

- If a deed of access is in place, make sure you have a copy for your personal records as this provides you with the right to obtain company information should there be any litigation during the seven-year period following your departure from the board. You would also hope that the company continues its directors' and officers' liability insurance during this period.

- It also a courtesy for you to meet with the CEO and other relevant staff to say goodbye and thank them for their efforts during your time on the board.

While I have indicated you should provide your resignation to the chairmen and company secretary, there may be circumstances where you bypass this and lodge your resignation directly with ASIC. This may occur when the board does not want to accept your resignation and refuses to process it or you are concerned that the company secretary will not forward the details to ASIC for some reason.

If the relationship between yourself and the other directors has broken down completely, you may wish to bypass any contact with them (perhaps for legal reasons) and lodge your resignation at the nearest ASIC office. If you do this, at least post a copy of your letter of resignation to the chairman or company secretary to ensure they know what action you have taken. I would only recommend doing method in extreme circumstances and where communication has broken down completely.

It is more likely that the board and you regret your departure and you leave on good terms. If this is the case, I would encourage you to stay connected with the key players from that board, even on a social basis. Recognise that the remaining directors will no longer be in a position to discuss confidential company information with you, but you will continue to enjoy each other's social company.

If you are looking to develop a wider range of board appointments, all these contacts and networks are useful and should be maintained where appropriate. I have found over the years that I've been able to connect with people for a variety of reasons through my various links to different boards and the people on them.

Depending on the company, you may have had some of your board fees paid into superannuation and you will need to make sure that this is finalised and up to date before your departure. Some companies also provide for a retirement or ex gratia payment on leaving the board and this is usually linked to your years of service. If this is the case, you will need to finalise this with the company accountant and by agreement with the chairman. You will probably find you have a continuing interest in the company of which you have been a director. While you will you now be an outsider looking in, you will still gain satisfaction from seeing the company continue to grow and succeed knowing that you had a small part to play in that.

It is for these contributions that you can make to companies that we need you as a director.

Chapter 20
Why We Need You

Too often the media portray company directors as overpaid people having long lunches at the expense of the shareholders. While there are no doubt some directors who have failed in doing their job and caused corporate collapses and loss to shareholders, these have been small in number. Human nature is such that in any given group of people, you will find a small number of bad eggs who let the side down. It's therefore unfair to highlight these at the expense of the reputation of the ninety-nine per cent of directors who work hard to look after shareholders' interests.

Those commentators who have never been a director have little understanding of the level of liability and risk that goes with the job and the long hours involved in being a company director. If you are a director of a company you always know that whatever happens, 'the buck stops here.' It's probably a bit easier for an executive director as people see them working in the company every day and don't question what they are being paid.

For non-executive directors it's a little harder as people see them attend a board meeting once a month and equate that amount of time to their fees. What they don't see are the hours between board meetings spent on a wide range of activities that go with the role and the liability that exists for them 365 days a year. I am not trying to justify or defend directors' fees, but simply trying to provide a wider understanding about remuneration levels for boards.

While a small number of directors let their shareholders down, most boards work extremely hard to protect shareholders' interests and grow their wealth. In the case of not-for-profit boards, directors are more likely to be unpaid and also put long volunteer hours into that entity by working for the wider community. A director of a government board is also contributing to the community by ensuring that the government entity provides a range of services to the wider community and perhaps some dividend revenue back to the taxpayer. Directors of family-owned companies don't only create wealth for the family shareholders, but usually provide employment for a large number of people in the local community for their consumer customers.

Yet we very rarely hear about these thousands of directors in of these types of organisations, quietly doing their job to the best of their ability. These are directors who guide small enterprises into significant commercial organisations, creating jobs for more and more people. These are the directors who ensure companies pay significant amounts of taxation that governments can use for the benefit of the wider economy. These are the directors of companies that manufacture consumer goods we all want or provide services we all need.

Some of these directors lead companies that eventually expand overseas and develop international operations and create a global presence for our country and perhaps export goods or services to the rest of the world. These are directors who have acted honestly and with integrity to fulfil their fiduciary duties and have acted in good faith at all times on behalf of the shareholders or members.

It is these companies, whether they have operated in the private or government sector or as not-for-profit entities, that have contributed and will continue to contribute to the economic growth of our nation. These directors are often faced with making extremely difficult and complex decisions on a regular basis in order to ensure the shareholders' interests are safeguarded.

Despite all this, we don't hear much about them in the public domain.

By now you probably think that I am a paid defender or apologist for company directors. I am not. I just happen to have observed over many years the difference that company directors have made to their organisations and the wider community.

*   *   *

So why do we need you?

The liability framework that exists today for company directors deters many people wanting to take on the role if offered. Others simply have no interest in being a director or don't understand what the role is.

The demand for a higher standard of skills has shrunk the pool of available talent for corporate boardrooms. In years gone by it was often the case that you saw the same directors on many boards because the gene pool was relatively small. The good news is that that trend is reversing as more and more younger people with the appropriate skills and interest are stepping up for consideration for board appointments.

The fact that you have read this book indicates you have some interest in being a company director. If that's the case, then we need you to make yourself available for board appointments, now or in the future.

As the number of companies continues to grow in a wide range of industries and sectors, so the demand for more and more skilled directors will also grow.

We have all seen the debate about the lack of women around board tables and the so-called glass ceiling. I'm pleased to say the past trend of small numbers of women serving as directors is also changing. This as least means both halves of the population will be available for future board appointments as men and women bring their unique sets of talents to company boardrooms and senior management positions.

Australia has been lucky to be a country with a high standard of living and some of the best economic growth seen in the world. I don't think I'm drawing too long a bow when I say company directors have had a major part to play in such economic growth and standards of living. We now have one of the largest populations of shareholders on a per capita basis in almost any country in the Western world. These range from mum-and-dad investors to large institutions and all of them need capable directors to sit on their behalf and look after their interests.

The thousands of companies with directors who are in the business of making a profit contribute to the economy by way of increased tax payments and dividends to shareholders that flow through to the wider community.

So, you want to be a company director? I am glad that you do and I hope that you now see why we need you.

I also hope you have gained something from reading this book, whether you are an experienced director or someone looking forward to your very first board appointment. This was never intended to be a textbook but simply a sharing of my experiences as a director over the years. Like all my fellow directors, I am only human and have made mistakes as a board member and sometimes got it wrong.

What I have tried to do, as I'm sure most directors do, is to get it right more times than not. I have derived a huge amount of satisfaction from sitting on boards of a wide range of companies. While I've had a lot of fun on various boards, I have also been through some difficult times having to grapple with complex issues and decisions. I just keep remembering that experience is the best teacher you can have.

I have tried to paint a balanced picture with all the plusses and minuses that go with the life of a director. I hope I haven't put you off wanting to join a board but instead provided a realistic picture of what you can expect. I have many great memories of my time on boards of directors. If you only enjoy it half as much as I have, then I am sure you won't regret it.

Thanks again for reading the book and every success in your career as a company director in the future. What I have tried to do, knowing that you have read this book, is provide some useful insights once you have realised 'So you want to be a company director'!